MILLION DOLLAR AGENT

The Proven Playbook To Build a Real Estate Empire

MILLION DOLLAR AGENT

The Proven Playbook To Build a Real Estate Empire

NICK MCLEAN

Copyright © 2023
Written by Nick McLean

Cover Artist Julie Hodgins
Book Designer Julie Hodgins
Copy Editor Chandi Lyn
Proofreaders Jamie Harmon and Brandy Vickery

ISBN: 979-8-218-21198-1

DEDICATION

To my loving wife Emily,
my dear parents and sister,
and my beloved daughter, Addalyn.

This book is dedicated to you,
the pillars of strength in my life.

CONTENTS

Dedication   *v*

Table of Contents   *vii*

Foreword   *ix*

Acknowledgments   *xi*

Introduction The Playbook   xiii

Chapter 1 Welcome   1

Chapter 2 Growth and Success   7

Chapter 3 Creating a Clear Vision   19

Chapter 4 Common Purpose   27

Chapter 5 Pinpointing Success   37

Chapter 6 Streamlining the Chain of Command   51

Chapter 7 Compensating Your Sales Team   61

Chapter 8 Geometric Growth   73

Chapter 9 Fee Structures   81

Chapter 10 Minimizing Risk   89

Chapter 11 Unique Selling Proposition   101

Chapter 12 Winning the Listing   113

Chapter 13 Optimizing the Buyer Sales Process   135

Chapter 14 Building a Strong Foundation   149

Chapter 15 High Performers   159

Chapter 16 Creating Raving Fans   173

Chapter 17 Building a Dream Team   189

Chapter 18 The Financials   201

Chapter 19 Building a Powerful Culture   211

Conclusion The Wrap-Up   219

References   223

About The Author   225

FOREWORD

I met Nick McLean five years ago when he reached out to discuss my coaching program. Twenty minutes into the conversation, we discovered a mutual desire to be the best version of ourselves; not just in business but in everything we do.

By that point in his life, Nick had already established a business that dominated his marketplace and was well on his way to building wealth through smart and disciplined investments. Like all high achievers, he knew there was more he could accomplish and was actively seeking that slight edge over his competition. I agreed to accept him into my program.

As is the case with all of my coaching clients, the teacher is ever the student—but Nick was more.

Nick has a background as one of the youngest 747 pilots in history. He helped an airline actually become an airline. He even helped write pilot training manuals. Because of this, the systems, processes, and checklists inside his real estate industry are unlike anything I have seen before.

Nick also never forgot those early days of struggle. The rise-and-grind of getting his business up and running informed his steps. He is intimately aware of that one spot in business most never breakthrough when it comes to building a team—

the messy middle. (In real estate, this is the space where team leaders are trying to grow their business while still out taking listings and working with buyers.)

Needless to say, Nick more than broke through. He built a life and business that allows him to wrap up his workday by 11 am so he can spend time with his family and pursue his interest in mountain bike racing while simultaneously holding a 20% market share and a 7-figure net income year after year.

Over the years, I discovered Nick's passion to give back to the real estate industry. He wants to support other leaders in building their businesses, allowing them to experience their hopes, dreams, and desires. Because of this, the natural progression was for Nick to take his proven formula and framework to team leaders throughout the world. He now transfers his knowledge to thousands of leaders through speaking, online courses, and one-on-one coaching sessions.

For the past three years, his formula and step-by-step solutions have had a massive impact on up-and-coming team leaders along with some of the most elite and accomplished team leaders in the world.

Nick doesn't need or want the attention that goes with publishing a book. But for a man who has accomplishments at the highest level, it's only fitting he reveals it all here in this book.

Jon Cheplak

ACKNOWLEDGMENTS

Emily, your unwavering support and love have been the foundation that has allowed me to pursue our burning passion for adventure. To my parents and sister, thank you for your constant support, and for sacrificing so much to give me the opportunity to explore, take risks, and pursue the calling of mastery in a wide range of skills available in life. Addalyn, the love and the joy that you bring to my life are the driving forces that push me to work hard and commit myself to serving others.

To all my mentors in business, and to my coach and friend, Jon Cheplak, I couldn't have done this without you. Thank you for your invaluable support, wisdom, and guidance. Your mentorship has been instrumental in shaping my career and life.

INTRODUCTION

THE PLAYBOOK

Learning what it takes to build
a million-dollar business.

Million Dollar Agent is a comprehensive guide for all real estate professionals. Whether you are a solo agent looking to improve sales and client relationships or a team leader looking to build your team and profits, you will get something from the following pages.

This is not a book about theory. It is not based on interviews. This book is straight from the trenches and is filled with actionable strategies that have been battle-tested and proven effective by many agents all over the U.S.

In the following pages, I will show you how I went from being a solo agent to building a top team where—in a town of under 100,000 people—we have held as much as 20% of the market share. In addition to running my team, I now coach real estate agents around the country on how to do exactly what I did. I have generated over $35,000,000 in commissions, sold over five thousand properties, and have seen steady increases in profit every year, even during housing downturns. I have distilled a decade of experience into foundational concepts that can be easily duplicated by agents and team leaders alike.

Regardless of your real estate goals, this book offers valuable insights on how to create a vision, culture, and core philosophies, as well as lead generation techniques, risk referrals, the listing process, and our buyer conversion process. This book not only teaches you how to grow your business ethically, but it also shows you how to protect your profit.

CHAPTER 1

WELCOME

Working your way to the top.

In this chapter, I will explain what you can expect to learn from this book, why I am motivated to teach people to succeed, and what to watch for as you read.

A successful real estate team is not simply a group of agents handling leads; it is a well-orchestrated division of labor that allows individuals to specialize in specific areas of the real estate operation. This specialization enables each team member to perform at a higher level than they could if they were tasked with handling every aspect of the business alone. To reach the pantheon of the top 1% of the top 1%, you have to master all aspects of running a successful sales and marketing company.

> **Mastery:** Notice, I did not say *real estate company*—real estate is what you do but your business is sales and marketing.

When I started my real estate team in 2012—after a four-year run as a solo agent working 10-hour days, seven days a week—there were no blueprints or established guidelines for team structures in the real estate industry. At that time, teams were still struggling to find footing in a predominantly solo-agent-driven market. Major online portals weren't as dominant as they are today, and laws and regulations had not yet evolved to effectively support team leaders in overseeing their agents. I established my own brokerage to overcome these challenges and ensure compliance with Washington State licensing requirements.

> **Framework:** Most of us don't need to go to this level, but doing so gave me insights into having total control

over all business areas. It is an important business lesson to learn that control is one of the key parts of owning a business. Most agents and teams don't have total control, and that limits their growth and speed to make effective decisions.

As a real estate agent looking to make the leap into the multi-million-dollar realm, you likely have numerous questions and concerns. Maybe even fears. This book will serve as a comprehensive guide, addressing the key concerns and curiosities team leaders may have as they embark on their journey.

Throughout the chapters, I will provide practical answers to the following questions:

- What is the ideal framework for a million-dollar agent, and how can I adapt it to suit my business model?
- How can I establish an efficient team structure that encourages growth and success in my real estate agency?
- What are the core philosophies and principles that drive the success of million-dollar agents?
- Which marketing strategies have proven most effective for top-tier agents, and how can I implement them in my own business?
- How can I create a repeatable listing system to streamline my processes and boost my agency's performance?
- What are the best practices for converting potential buyers into loyal clients?
- How do I set up a functional administration system to optimize my team's workflow and productivity?

- To excel in the competitive real estate industry, what essential areas of expertise do I need to invest in for myself and my team?
- How can I define and deliver a top-notch client experience that sets me and my agency apart from the competition?
- What strategies should I employ to recruit and retain the best talent for my team? As a solo agent, how do I become top talent?
- How do I analyze and break down the financial metrics and key performance indicators that will help me gauge my agency's progress toward becoming a million-dollar enterprise?

As you read through this book, you'll gain insights, tips, and strategies that have propelled others to great success. By the end of your journey, you will have a better understanding of what it takes to build your own million-dollar real estate empire.

HOW TO USE THIS BOOK

As you read, pay extra attention to **framework, mastery,** and **$1M** notes. The information highlighted in these sections are insights into building your business like a seasoned professional. **Framework** is where you will learn foundational principals that all agents should know. **Mastery** will help you build a deeper understanding of the real estate business. **$1M** is where you will find notes on how to set yourself apart from the competition; it's what the pros do.

At the end of each chapter, you will also find **next steps.** These are actionable steps you can take to implement the information you learned in that chapter.

By following the frameworks, strategies, and tools presented in this book, you will be well-equipped to create the most profitable real estate team in your marketplace.

If you're looking to take your real estate business to the next level, *Million Dollar Agent: The Proven Playbook To Build a Real Estate Empire* is the book for you.

CHAPTER 2

GROWTH AND SUCCESS

A look at our team's
timeline and statistics.

---

*In this chapter, I will illustrate the history
of my journey from an unknown solo
agent in a small town to a successful real
estate team in a new marketplace.*

As a 19-year-old college sophomore, I never could have imagined the path my life would take. I couldn't decide on a major and took a summer job at Carlile Transportation in Anchorage, Alaska, made famous by the TV show *Ice Road Truckers*.

I spent long, tiring nights working in the water bay—pressure washing the dirt and grime off of eighteen-wheelers that had made their thousand-mile journeys to Prudhoe Bay. During these seemingly endless nights, I had an epiphany: I wanted to become an airline pilot.

My first step was enrolling in aviation school. While there, I worked hard to earn a degree in business management over the next two years. Eager to continue my education, I attended Embry-Riddle Aeronautical University, where I spent another two years acquiring all the necessary pilot licenses.

Undeterred, I moved to Miami and began working for Focus Air Cargo. For two more years, I honed my skills and gained valuable industry experience. Then, six years after making that initial decision while hosing down big rigs in Alaska, I became the youngest Boeing 747 pilot in North America.

To my 19-year-old brain, six years would have seemed like an eternity. If I had known the amount of effort it would take, I'm not sure I would have begun the journey. But looking back, the time went by quickly, and the achievements along the way were more life-changing than I could have anticipated.

> **Framework:** It's important to remember that thinking big and focusing on the long term can yield incredible results.

As a real estate agent, the same principles apply. Building a successful team may not happen overnight, but with patience, perseverance, and a long-term commitment, you can accomplish far more than you initially imagined. Instead of sprinting toward short-term goals, embrace the journey and focus on endurance. When you take the time to build a strong foundation, the sky's the limit.

My real estate career over the short run fell short of my expectations and over the long run exceeded my wildest dreams. Think big and think long-term.

MY REAL ESTATE JOURNEY

From 2008–2012, I sold real estate as a solo agent in the small town of Lake Chelan. As my business grew, my broker wasn't positioned to support my goal of starting a team. He encouraged me to get my designated broker license. I followed his advice and did just that.

Within ninety days, I was licensed to go out on my own, and our team opened its doors on March 2nd, 2012. Our market was the town of Wenatchee, WA. At the time, it had a population of 53,000, and I was the new guy in an established marketplace.

In 2012, our team sold 101 properties for a total revenue of $443,000. This was a solid start for our new business, but we knew that we needed to continue to grow and improve to be successful in the long term.

Our team consisted of:

- One Team Leader (TL)
- Five Buyer Specialists
- One Assistant (Personal Assistant to TL, Listing Coordinator, Closing Coordinator duties)

In 2013, we sold 201 properties for a total revenue of $966,229. This was a significant increase over the previous year and showed that our business was starting to gain traction in the local market. This is also the year I stepped away from working with buyers.

Our team consisted of:

- One Team Leader (who also acted as a Listing Specialist)
- Six Buyer Specialists
- One Assistant (who acted as the Personal Assistant to the TL, Listing Coordinator, and performed Closing Coordinator duties)

In 2014, we sold 252 properties for a total revenue of $1,476,233. This was an even greater increase from the previous year and demonstrated that our reputation and brand were gaining recognition in the area.

Our team consisted of:

- One Team Leader (who also acted as a Listing Specialist)
- Eight Buyer Specialists
- One Listing Coordinator
- One Closing Coordinator

In 2015, we sold 290 properties for a total revenue of $2,002,402. We passed a significant milestone and felt that we were doing something right.

Our team consisted of:

- One Team Leader (who also acted as a Listing Specialist)
- One Listing Partner
- Ten Buyer Specialists
- One Listing Coordinator
- One Closing Coordinator

In 2016, we sold 380 properties for a total revenue of $2,633,084. This was a record year for our team, and we demonstrated that we had become a major player in the local real estate market.

Our team consisted of:

- One Team Leader (who also acted as a Listing Specialist)
- One Listing Partner
- Fourteen Buyer Specialists
- One Listing Coordinator
- One Closing Coordinator
- One Inside Sales Associate (ISA)

In 2017, we sold 386 properties for a total revenue of $2,725,410. This was another successful year for our team, showing that our business continued to grow and thrive.

Our team consisted of:

- One Team Leader (who also acted as a Listing Specialist)
- One Listing Associate to support the TL
- One Listing Partner
- Sixteen Buyer Specialists
- One Listing Coordinator
- One Closing Coordinator
- One ISA

In 2018, we sold 412 properties for a total revenue of $3,225,062. We established ourselves as one of the top-producing teams in the area. This is the year I stepped out of production as the team leader and focused on marketing, recruiting, and expansion.

Our team consisted of:

- One Team Leader (who also acted as a Listing Specialist)
- One Listing Associate to support the TL
- One Listing Partner
- Sixteen Buyer Specialists
- One Listing Coordinator
- One Closing Coordinator
- One ISA
- One Full-time Photographer

In 2019, we sold 398 properties for a total revenue of $3,225,062. Although the number of properties sold was slightly lower than the previous year, the revenue remained at the same level, demonstrating the strength of our team and our ability to sell higher-priced properties. This year we also opened a property management company.

Our team consisted of:

- One Team Leader
- Two Listing Partners
- Eighteen Buyer Specialists
- One Listing Coordinator
- One Closing Coordinator
- Two ISAs
- One Full-time Photographer

In 2020, we sold 528 properties for a total revenue of $4,908,508. This was driven by the high demand for properties due to low-interest rates and a strong economy.

Our team consisted of:

- One Team Leader
- One Director of Sales
- Six Listing Partners
- Thirty-two Buyer Specialists
- One Listing Coordinator
- One Closing Coordinator
- Two ISAs
- One Full-time Photographer

In 2021, we sold 446 properties for a total revenue of $5,032,880. This was another strong year for our team, despite the challenges posed by the ongoing pandemic. Our team's ability to adapt and pivot to meet the changing market conditions helped us grow.

Our team consisted of:

- One Team Leader
- One Director of Sales
- Eight Listing Partners
- Thirty-two Buyer Specialists
- One Listing Coordinator
- One Closing Coordinator
- Two ISAs
- One Full-time Photographer

These statistics demonstrate the impressive growth and success that teams can achieve in any marketplace when they focus and persevere. While many teams focus on goals over a single year, they often fail to see the impact they can have over a decade. I didn't want to win one championship, I wanted to win several; becoming a dynasty.

Even if you aren't looking to build a real estate team, it is still good to understand how they function and most of the principles in the following pages apply equally to individual agents and teams.

Mastery: I recommend all team leaders achieve the highest level of licensing available. You are not only a team leader, you are the thought and regulatory leader. You must know how everything works, even at a franchise or office. As a leader, you may be able to delegate the tasks of compliance but don't think you are not responsible for your team's compliance. As our team grew and my agents became more experienced, I paid for them to get the highest level of licensing.

Outline your growth strategies and organization structures with the following questions:

- What are your short and long-term goals for your real estate business?
- Who are your ideal clients, and what are their needs and preferences? Where do they live, what do they do and where do they go outside of their home? We will go over this in Chapter 5.
- How do you plan to differentiate your team or yourself from your competition?
- What are the key skills and traits you are looking for in new team members?
- How will you manage and distribute leads among team members?
- What systems and processes will you put in place to ensure efficient communication and collaboration within the team?
- How will you measure the success of your team and individual team members?

- How will you stay up-to-date with industry trends and changes in the marketplace?
- What kind of support and resources will you offer team members to help them grow and succeed?
- How will you foster a positive team environment that is conducive to encourage the team member to choose to be productive?

NEXT STEPS:
HOW TO BUILD GROWTH AND SUCCESS

- Start with a clear vision for your team and its future and make it visible. See Chapter 3.
- Identify your three strengths, weaknesses, greatest opportunities, and biggest threats.
- Create a detailed organizational chart to clarify roles and responsibilities within the team. Build an organizational chart for how your team will look in two, five, and ten years.
- Implement systems and processes that help streamline communication and collaboration.
- Set clear performance expectations and regularly evaluate team members' progress.
- Invest in training and development programs for yourself and your team.
- Gather feedback from team members and clients to improve your services and processes.
- Stay organized and focused on your goals but be flexible and adaptable as the market and your team evolves. Estab-

lish a team that is resistant to major changes over ten-year cycles. This isn't a sprint.

- Surround yourself with experienced and knowledgeable advisors who can help you make informed decisions. Seek out and join like-minded team leaders and broker-owners in a mastermind setting. Have a business coach who knows your industry inside and out to guide you.
- Celebrate your successes and learn from your failures. A healthy team celebrates wins and works through losses. Don't pretend there is a perfect team, seek to create a committed team.

In the following chapters, I will show you exactly what we did and how we did it.

CHAPTER 3

CREATING A CLEAR VISION

Developing a mission statement and core values to drive success in your business.

In this chapter, I will show you how to use your mission statement and core values to guide decision-making and differentiate your team in the competitive real estate market.

In 2005, after graduating in the top three from the aviation school, I stood at the crossroads of my career. With my commercial airline license and DC-9 type rating, I was eager to embark on my journey as a commercial pilot and build my flight hours to become a Captain. I had three job opportunities, including interviews with AirTran and Atlantic Southeast Airlines, both offering instant jet airline experience.

However, I chose the path less traveled and joined Focus Air Cargo as an apprentice. Why? Because of their inspiring vision and mission.

Focus Air Cargo, an unproven airline with only two Boeing 747s, had ambition. Their goal was to become the number one international airline in the world, growing from a fleet of two planes to hundreds of 747s within five years. The vision captivated me, and I wanted to be a part of something extraordinary. It was not just about tangible rewards but about being challenged and doing my best work.

My experience at Focus Air Cargo taught me that people are drawn to a powerful vision and mission statement. They want to be part of something bigger than themselves; an organization that pushes the boundaries and challenges them to grow. As a real estate agent, I understood that having a clear vision would help me stay focused on my goals and attract like-minded individuals who shared the same passion and aspirations.

So, in 2013, we took our staff of seven people on a two-day offsite retreat in Seattle, WA, with the sole purpose of clarifying our purpose, mission, and values. During this offsite, we identified the core values that were important to us as a team and as individuals.

We emerged with a clear mission statement and core values that have served as our guiding light in all aspects of our business—including hiring, firing, and decision-making.

MISSION STATEMENT

"Be the leading real estate experts of choice as leaders in the real estate industry, to our clients, and within our communities."

This statement guides our actions and decision-making and reminds us of why we do what we do.

CORE VALUES

- We support team members' excellence and happiness.
- We value family, health, and community.
- We pursue growth and learning.
- We are dependable, passionate, and determined.

At Nick McLean Real Estate Group, we believe in teamwork and that together, everyone achieves more.

These values are not just words on a piece of paper, they are the foundation of our team culture and are integral to our success. They are used as a filter in our hiring process and serve as a benchmark for performance evaluations.

As a result, we have experienced an incredible decade of market-share growth. Our top 20% market-share points directly back to this one offsite meeting that gave us the clarity of thought to focus on goals that mattered to us.

Developing a clear mission statement and core values is crucial for any real estate agent, especially teams. By having a clear and compelling vision and guiding principles, you and your team can differentiate yourselves from the competition and experience sustained growth.

Once you have clarified your mission statement and defined your core values, you have to implement them. If your team constantly breaks from your mission and values, there is no reason to have created them in the first place. We often see companies that point to their mission statement and say, "Look! We are good!" only to turn around and betray those same values. They write bad contracts, push people around, and undermine their credibility.

If your goal is to create an open culture where people can ask questions and share ideas but gossip about Jaqi's ideas or dismiss Brian's questions as pointless, then your mission and goals are not serving as anything more than a weekend away at a retreat.

> **Framework:** Your mission statement and core values are a guiding light for tough decision-making, such as hiring and firing and differentiation in the competitive market. What your team values will show up in their actions, either good or bad, so pay attention.

If you already have a mission statement and defined core values, congratulations! They should serve as a unifying anthem for your team. If they don't, figure out why and work to fix it.

If you don't have either of these documents—or need to revise the ones you do have—there are many books, blogs, and podcasts dedicated to this aspect of business. A few of my favorites are, *Good to Great* by Jim Collins, *BE 2.0* by James Collins, *The Culture Code: The Secrets of Highly Successful Groups* by Daniel Coyle, and *Drive: The Surprising Truth About What Motivates Us* by Daniel H. Pink.

NEXT STEPS:
HOW TO CREATE A CLEAR VISION

- Establish core values and purpose by determining the values that guide your team's actions and decisions. These values should be non-negotiable and consistently upheld by all team members. Meet with your team (or by yourself) and answer the following questions:

  - What are the principles that guide your decision-making?
  - How do I want my employees to behave and interact with each other and clients?
  - What makes a meaningful work environment?
  - How can I encourage ethical and responsible behavior within the company?
  - What are the non-negotiable standards?

- How can our core values promote a positive company culture?
- How can our core values help us make tough decisions and stay on track when faced with challenges?
- How do our core values align with the company's mission and vision?

- Conduct a Strengths, Weaknesses, Opportunities, and Threats (SWOT) analysis. Assessing your team's SWOT in the real estate marketplace will help identify where your team excels, areas to improve, potential growth opportunities, and external factors that may impact your success. It is important to return to this analysis as the marketplace will change and you and your team will have to adapt to new opportunities and threats.

- Create a 5-year Goal. Jim Collins emphasizes the importance of setting a Big Hairy Audacious Goal (BHAG), an ambitious long-term goal that might seem impossible (2004). This goal will create a sense of excitement and challenge among team members.

- Develop a clear mission statement. Review your core values, purpose, and 5-year goal, then use them to craft a clear and concise mission statement that defines what your team aims to accomplish. Ensure that this mission statement is easily understood and can be articulated by all team members.

- Establish a culture of procedural discipline. It is important to have your agents focus on the process over results because the distance between what works and the result is so far apart. By following the procedure, you will see consistent results over time. Ensure your team members consistently adhere to your processes and values and hold each other accountable for their actions, decisions, and performance.

- Assemble a team of strong, capable leaders who are committed to the vision and possess the skills necessary to drive the team's success. Cultivate a culture of mentorship and ongoing professional development to continuously strengthen your leadership team.

- Share your company vision with all team members, ensuring everyone understands their role in achieving the team's goals. Continuously reinforce the vision through team meetings, performance evaluations, and team-building activities.

- As your team progresses, evaluate your vision to ensure that it remains relevant and continues to drive the team toward success. Be open to refining your vision as the real estate market evolves and your team grows and adapts.

- Acknowledge and celebrate the milestones and accomplishments achieved by your team. Recognizing progress and rewarding effort will create a positive atmosphere and help maintain motivation toward achieving the team's vision.

Use your mission statement and core values to direct your decision-making. If you don't have them, get them. If they aren't serving you, change them.

CHAPTER 4

COMMON PURPOSE

Building strong teams through shared belief systems.

---

*In this chapter, we will discuss
the importance of a common purpose and
how you can use it to build stronger teams.*

As a child, I was passionate about sports. Basketball, football, baseball—you name it, I played it. For me, the allure of team sports lay in collectiveness, camaraderie, and unwavering commitment to achieving a common goal. The selflessness of a team creates freedom, allowing individual expression to flourish once you've earned the trust of those around you.

My experiences playing on top-performing teams and dysfunctional ones taught me a valuable lesson; the secret to a high-achieving team is found in the team-level beliefs that the individuals adopt. These group beliefs guide personal behavior and foster an identity that can transform average people with ordinary expectations into individuals with a higher sense of belief and character.

This realization came into sharp focus during my time at Embry Riddle Aeronautical University—the best civil aeronautical university in the history of the world. The power of Embry Riddle is the rich history of developing world-class aviators, who are known for their supreme flight discipline and airmanship.

When you join this group, you immediately gain a sense that you need to elevate your standards in order to fit in. As you do, one of three things will happen: the collective group will pull you up to their level, you will self-select to remove yourself, or the group will protect the standards and culture and demand that leadership removes you. The people who remain are aligned with the higher standards where the group can hold everyone accountable.

Low standards come from a lack of clarity on the group's expectation of exceptional performance.

I was fortunate enough to have the opportunity to fly with Air Force fighter pilots who exhibited unparalleled skill and precision. They were better pilots not because they flew fighter jets, but because they belonged to an elite group that instilled a powerful belief system within them. When those same pilots work for a dysfunctional airline, they build resentment and look for the first opportunity to leave. Those who stay are reduced to average pilots.

As I embarked on my journey as a real estate team leader, I carried these lessons with me. I knew that adopting a strong set of beliefs and fostering an identity of excellence would be crucial to my success in the competitive world of real estate. Just like the elite fighter pilots and the top-performing sports teams I had been a part of, I aimed to create an environment that would cultivate success.

In today's fast-paced business environment, having a solid belief system is a critical component in building strong and successful teams. Your belief system is separate from your mission statement and vision. Think of it as your team's operating system for how to act and behave. These differ from Core Values because they are specific beliefs that drive behavior and can cross broad areas and situations internally and externally in the field.

Our team's first belief is *Mastery*. In our team, it is essential for each employee to continuously increase their knowledge, skills, and abilities to a high level of mastery. This belief is reflected in our commitment to provide ongoing training and resources for our team members to learn and gain expertise.

This belief system requires team members to reflect on past performances and be open to feedback. Without the pursuit of mastery, reflection, and growth are not necessarily demanded. To build mastery, I encourage my team to study a particular skill or subject until they feel like they could teach it. Then I encourage them to learn some more.

Next, we believe in *Putting our Clients First*. We understand that our clients are the reason we are in business. We always keep this in mind, in everything we do. We prioritize their needs above our own and work as a team to deliver the best possible experience for them.

Without this belief system, agents and individuals will put their own interests ahead of the client's best interest. This can result in early success and sales but sacrifices the long-term value of the client relationship.

Teamwork is another important belief system for our team. We believe that together, everyone can achieve more. This is why we encourage collaboration and open communication within our team, ensuring everyone works together toward a common goal. Without teamwork as a belief system, your company will lack effective communication and collaboration.

Team members play a vital role in any organization and we believe in developing leadership skills at all levels. Our belief system of *Leaders* outlines the five levels of leadership, providing a roadmap for each employee to grow and develop their leadership skills. John Maxwell's book *Five Levels of Leadership* shaped this belief system. When you have this operating system, you see real value in everyone's leadership growth.

> **$1M:** The biggest difference between a $1,000,000 team and a $5,000,000 team is not their lead source; it is the quantity and quality of leadership within the organization.

Abundance is another belief system we hold. Taking positive action creates opportunities for everyone. This belief drives us to take risks and pursue new ideas. We are always looking for ways to create abundance for our clients, team, and company.

Being accountable and committed is also important to our team. This is reflected in our belief system of *Pilot in Command* (PIC). We understand that as leaders, it is our responsibility to take 100% accountability and make decisions with a zero-excuse mentality.

Let me explain: every flight in America has a PIC. The PIC is one person who is solely responsible for the safety and performance of the flight. The PIC must be known and identified before each flight. Failure to identify the PIC in each real estate transaction could result in total failure and loss of your license because there is no acting and accountable fiduciary. In other words, the client doesn't have representation. Your team needs to know who they work for, and your client needs to know who their agent is, at all times.

Having clarity is essential in any endeavor, and we believe in knowing the goal and the why behind it. Our belief system of *Clarity* ensures that we understand the purpose behind our actions and work together toward a common goal.

Finally, our belief system of *Action* recognizes that by knowing what we want to achieve, the how will fall into place. We encourage our team to take action, be proactive, and make things happen.

Our belief systems play a crucial role in shaping our company culture and building strong teams. By having a shared set of beliefs and values, we are able to work together toward a common goal and create a positive and productive work environment.

The following questions will help any agent or team leader identify and gain clarity on a set of belief systems to adopt and follow:

- What values and principles are most important to me, both personally and professionally?
- What do I believe sets our team apart from other real estate teams in the market?
- What qualities do I want our team to be known for in the industry?
- How do I define success, and how can our team collectively work toward achieving it?

- What are my expectations for team members' behavior, work ethic, and attitude toward clients and each other?
- How can our team contribute positively to our community and the environment?
- What is our team's mission, and how can it guide our daily actions and long-term goals?
- What types of relationships do I want to foster with clients, and how can our team consistently deliver on those expectations?
- How can our team support each other's growth, development, and overall well-being?
- What are the non-negotiable standards of integrity and professionalism that every team member must adhere to?

Here is a complete list of our team's belief systems:

- **Mastery:** We strive to continuously learn and improve our knowledge, skills, and abilities to reach a high level of mastery. The emphasis is on personal growth and development, and the idea is that the more an individual learns, the better they can perform their tasks.
- **Client First:** We place the client's needs and wants ahead of the individual's. Our customer-centric approach recognizes that the success of the business is directly tied to the satisfaction of our clients.
- **Teamwork:** We emphasize the power of collaboration and the idea that working together as a team can lead to greater results than working individually. It recognizes that each team member brings unique skills and perspectives and that pooling these resources can lead to better outcomes.

- **Leaders:** The 5 levels of leadership recognizes the importance of leadership in achieving success. It divides leadership into five levels, from basic to advanced, and encourages individuals to strive for mastery in each level.

- **Abundance:** We recognize that there is enough for everyone and that positive action creates opportunities for all. It encourages individuals to approach challenges and opportunities with an abundance mindset, believing that success is not limited and that there are always opportunities to grow and succeed.

- **Pilot in Command:** Our team places accountability and commitment at the forefront. We encourage individuals to take full responsibility for their actions and decisions and to lead with passion and determination.

- **Clarity:** We emphasize the importance of understanding each goal and the why behind it. Having a clear understanding of what is to be achieved can lead to greater motivation and success.

- **Action:** Knowing what to do is not enough; an individual must also take action, even when the how is not clear.

- **Logic:** We encourage individuals to approach challenges and opportunities with a well-trained and open mind, using common sense and intuition to make decisions. It recognizes that logical thinking can lead to better outcomes and encourages individuals to improve their ability to continuously think critically.

- **Beginner's Mind:** Continuous learning and being open to new knowledge and experiences encourages individuals to approach challenges and opportunities with curiosity and passion, recognizing that there is always more to learn and that growth is a process.

NEXT STEPS:
HOW TO BUILD A COMMON PURPOSE

- Start with a team brainstorming session. Gather your team and discuss which beliefs and values are important to them and how they align with the company's mission and vision. Encourage open discussion and idea sharing. If you need help, look for inspirational people and businesses, and understand their philosophies.
- Look for common themes and values that emerged from the brainstorming session. These will form the foundation of your shared belief system.
- Take the common themes and values and turn them into clear and concise statements. These statements should define your team's shared beliefs and values.
- Once you have defined your beliefs, clearly communicate them to the team. This can be done through a company-wide meeting, email, or other communication channels.
- Embed your beliefs in your day-to-day operations. Make sure your beliefs are integrated into all aspects of your business, from your recruitment process to your performance management system.
- Recognize and celebrate your team's successes and how they align with your shared belief system. This helps reinforce the importance of your beliefs and how they contribute to the team's success.

- Regularly evaluate your beliefs and make changes as needed. Ensure that they remain relevant and aligned with the team's needs and the company's mission and vision.

By following these steps, you can create a shared belief system that drives success and helps build strong teams. A shared belief system fosters a positive and productive work environment, encourages personal and professional growth, and aligns the team's efforts toward a common goal.

CHAPTER 5

PINPOINTING SUCCESS

How to create an ideal client and market profile.

In this chapter, I will show you how to maximize your marketing efforts and generate more leads by understanding your target client and market.

started my own real estate firm in 2012, and I was eager to make a name for myself. I invested tens of thousands of dollars into building the team, branding, and marketing materials. I even signed a three-year commercial lease for our office. Money was tight and I was desperate to get some cash flow. I was ready to work with anyone who walked through my door. Little did I know, this desperation would lead me to learn a valuable lesson the hard way.

Five months into our operation, a man entered my office. To protect his privacy, let's just call him John. John came to me with an unusual proposal. He claimed to have a house in a nice part of town, worth $750,000 and already had a buyer lined up. All he wanted from me was to write up the contract and handle the sale for a reduced commission of 1%, which amounted to $7,500. I found it strange that he'd choose to pay me rather than go directly to an attorney, but my desperation clouded my judgment, and I couldn't pass up the opportunity for a quick influx of cash. I accepted the offer.

As I drew up the contract, I couldn't shake my uneasy feeling about John. But my financial situation had me in a bind, and I was willing to overlook my instincts. The buyer agreed to the contract, and everything seemed to be going smoothly until their own property sale fell through, leaving them without the necessary funds to close on John's house. At this point, I'd only lost a few hours of work, and I thought it was a manageable setback. But then, things took a turn for the worse.

Without my knowledge, John had received a $50,000 payment from the buyer—outside of our agreement. The buyer believed it to be earnest money but John insisted it was non-refundable. In no time, the two parties were suing each other, and as the agent of record, I was dragged into the legal dispute. I was forced to spend time and money meeting with attorneys to resolve a situation I never wanted to be a part of.

This experience taught me a vital lesson about the importance of being selective in choosing clients. It's crucial to establish your ideal client profile and be clear about who you're unwilling to work with, no matter how enticing the commission may be. There are people you don't want to work with, and they will use money to lure you into compromising situations. Cheap people are cheap people; those who fire others will fire you; and those who give bad reviews to other agents will inevitably give you a bad review.

From that day on, I learned to look for warning signs and focus on serving clients who aligned with my values and vision. In the long run, it's the relationships built on trust and integrity that will create a successful business and a fulfilling career. So remember, never let desperation cloud your judgment, and always choose your clients wisely. To my knowledge, the owner kept the $50,000 and the buyers chose not to pursue the lawsuit any longer.

So, how do you protect yourself?

Let's first start with creating your ideal client profile.

Identifying your clientele is an essential step in creating a successful real estate business. This profile is a detailed description of your ideal customer. It includes information like age, income, location, and lifestyle.

To create an ideal client profile for your real estate team, start by analyzing your current customer base. Identify common characteristics. For example, you may notice that most of your clients are young professionals.

You can use online research tools, such as Google Analytics, to gather more information about your ideal client. Then use this data to determine the areas in which your clients are likely to live and the types of homes they are likely to be interested in buying.

Once you have a clear understanding of your ideal client base, you can tailor your marketing efforts to attract the right customers. For example, if your target clientele includes young professionals, you should focus your marketing efforts on social media platforms that are popular with this demographic. Those campaigns should use language that is familiar to that audience.

To help identify your target audience, I recommend Seth Godin's books *Purple Cow, The Dip,* and *This Is Marketing.* These all highlight the importance of understanding your audience and creating products and marketing campaigns that resonate with them. Donald Miller's book *Building a StoryBrand* focuses on understanding your audience and creating a compelling narrative that resonates with them. John Jantsch's book *Duct Tape Marketing* offers a comprehensive approach to marketing and includes advice on creating an ideal client profile.

Here are some prompts to help you determine your ideal client:

- Who is my current customer base?
- How did they hear about our team?

> **Mastery:** Ask every lead and client, "Who do we have to thank for referring you to our team?"

- What are the demographics of my target market?
- What target client gives my team energy and passion for serving?

> **Framework:** It isn't all about maximizing profit; you need an ideal client that maximizes your team's contribution energy!

- What are the common characteristics of my current clients?
- What areas do my ideal clients live in?
- What types of homes are my ideal clients interested in? What types of homes do my ideal clients own?
- What are their pain points?
- How can our team solve their pain and provide solutions?
- Which social media platforms are popular with my ideal client demographic?
- How can I tailor my marketing efforts to reach my ideal clients?
- What is the cost of my current marketing efforts and how many leads have they generated?

- What is the shortest drive time for potential clients to my office or properties?
- What areas have the lowest competition for real estate agents and teams?

As a team leader, identifying clients or team members you don't want to work with is also crucial for maintaining a healthy and successful work environment. There are times that saying no is a win for the team's long-term success.

Here are some questions you can ask yourself to help determine the kinds of clients you don't want to work with:

- Does this person share our team's values and vision?
- Do they have a history of difficult relationships with others in the industry? Look for patterns of negative behavior, such as frequent disputes or bad reviews. If their past interactions show a tendency for conflict or dissatisfaction, they may not be the best client for your team. You will notice these things when new clients approach your business. If they talk negatively about other agents, don't take any personal responsibility for what happened, have an overall disdain for real estate agents and the industry, and express how they could do it themselves, this is probably not a client you want to work with.
- Are they honest and transparent in their communication? Assess their communication style and whether they seem forthcoming with information. Clients who withhold information or are dishonest can become a huge headache for your team.

- Do they respect boundaries and the expertise of the agent? Determine if they're willing to listen and respect professional opinions. Those who consistently disregard boundaries or the expertise of others may create a toxic work environment.

- Are they flexible and open to compromise? Consider whether they're willing to make adjustments and adapt to changing circumstances. A person who is rigid and unwilling to compromise can hinder the team's ability to find creative solutions and move forward.

- Do they have realistic expectations? Evaluate if their expectations are reasonable, both in terms of the project's outcome and the team's capabilities. Clients with unrealistic expectations can lead to disappointment and strain on the team.

By asking these questions, you can better identify clients who may not be a good fit for your team. It's essential to prioritize your team's well-being and long-term success over the potential for short-term financial gains.

Now that you know your ideal client, let's identify your ideal market area and price point. To begin, determine the highest price-point areas and analyze the data on home sales in your area. Then, cross-reference the highest price point with those most likely to sell. I call this finding the sweet spot in the marketplace—the area with the highest price point and the properties that are most likely to sell.

> **Mastery:** A general rule of thumb to find the sweet spot is to look for areas that are 3%–10% above the average sales price in a given marketplace.

Don't underestimate throughput and sales cycles. You may want to sell a million-dollar property, but it could take two hundred days. In that same period, you could have sold five two-hundred-thousand-dollar properties. The same amount of money was sold but the lower price points gave you consistent cash flow.

There are times when luxury homes stay on the market longer than your listing-agreement terms. Any time the average days on the market exceed your listing term, you risk not getting paid. The higher the price point, the more likely you won't get paid. To counter this, extend your listing agreement terms. We use a one-year listing agreement; our competition uses six-month listings. We are proactive and get listing extensions with every price reduction.

> **Framework:** Don't wait until your listing is going to expire to get an extension. Add thirty to sixty days each time you do a price reduction.

> **$1M:** Be upfront with your client and never try to sneak things past them.

Next, you need to determine the areas with the lowest competition. Research the number of real estate agents and teams in your target market. Look for areas where there are fewer agents and teams, as these areas may have less competition. You can research the marketing strategies of other agents and teams in your target market to identify any gaps that you can fill with your unique approach. More agents means more competition, more pressure on commissions, and higher cost-per-lead. Sam Walton, the founder of Wal-Mart, would advise you to over-serve underserved markets.

Your local title and escrow company likely has access to this data. Simply ask them to run reports on different market areas and cross reference with sites like Zillow to see who sells homes in those areas.

Drive times matter. To determine the shortest drive times, use a mapping tool to measure the distance between potential clients' properties and your office or the properties you plan to show them. This will allow you to target potential clients who are in the closest proximity to your office, which can increase the likelihood of them becoming a client. Your team of agents will also have higher conversion rates in the areas they live and work. Their answer rates will be higher because they won't be worried it will be a long drive or they won't know anything about the property and neighborhood.

> **Mastery:** The longer the drive time, the lower the competition. We have dominated small towns for the last decade. Towns under five thousand people often don't have a local agent. And if they do, that agent isn't very good.

> When we go on a listing appointment, our clients are often happy that we even showed up because, in many of these towns, the local agents often bail. Because of this, we can charge a premium commission to set off the added time-to-service.

I know it is tempting to go wide in your market sandbox, but you should go deep. Going deep is like a tree's roots, and you want to set deep roots in communities. It is usually better to become the number-one agent in a community and neighborhood. When you get a listing, the initial goal is to sell the home, but that is not the ultimate goal. The ultimate goal is to let everyone know you are the go-to team when it comes to selling homes in this area. For your top communities, you need to support their events, non-profits, schools, and more. Be visible. Be the market maven for the community with market updates. We do market-update newsletters with videos each month for the top three communities we serve. We even send our newsletter as a press release to the local newspapers and media outlets.

Now that you have your client and market defined, you need to determine the lowest cost-per-lead. To calculate this, take the cost of your marketing efforts and divide that by the number of leads generated. This will give you an idea of which marketing strategies are the most cost-effective and where you should focus your efforts. The rule of thumb is the more top-funnel a lead is, the lower the cost. The lower the lead is in the funnel, the higher the cost.

Think of it this way. A Facebook lead is someone who was scrolling and saw a house for sale and clicked. They are 100% curious, but not committed. They search your site and you call. That is a top funnel. Now, think about a Zillow lead that has been searching for months to find a home. They find a house and click to talk to an agent. That is a lower funnel. I know what you are thinking; I will just buy Zillow leads. Well, you and everyone else, and that is why the price of that lead is 10–100x more. A top funnel lead could be pennies or dollars. A Zillow lead will be hundreds or thousands of dollars. Learn to generate your own leads and nurture them with follow-up automation into lower funnel leads.

You are a client manufacturing company. The difference is the time it takes to close. Have strategies for both types of leads.

NEXT STEPS:
HOW TO PINPOINT SUCCESS

- Conduct market research by analyzing market trends, historical sales data, and demographic information to identify areas you want to work in. Focus on areas with home values 3%–10% above the median to ensure profitable transactions. Your local title and escrow company can help pull this data, or you can use larger data collection companies like CoreLogic.
- Figure out where your agents live. Research their specific areas. This reduces travel time and increases the likelihood of successful lead conversion. (Sometimes this means hiring agents who live in specific/underserved areas.)

- Analyze turnover rates. Choose areas with higher-than-normal turnover rates, which indicates a potential for consistent business.
- Identify areas with less competition from mega agents with strong footholds in the market, allowing your team to easily build a more substantial presence.
- Select areas with lower costs to generate leads online, which helps maintain a healthy marketing budget.
- Develop marketing materials that emphasize your commitment and expertise as the local and predominant expert for the specific marketplace. Tailor these campaigns to the demographics and preferences of your ideal clients. Talk to marketing experts for advice. They know what they are doing. Trust them.
- Engage in community outreach by establishing strong relationships with local organizations, schools, and businesses to become a trusted expert in the community.
- Use Search Engine Optimization (SEO), social media, and content marketing to showcase your expertise and attract your ideal clients.
- Form strategic partnerships with professionals in related industries, such as mortgage brokers, attorneys, and home inspectors, to build your reputation and generate referrals. Walk around your town. Talk to business owners. The worst they can do is say "no".

Pinpointing success in the real estate industry requires a strategic approach. Understanding your ideal client profile and marketplace with specificity and clarity will drive your marketing, advertising, conversion, agent attraction, processes, and client experience.

Analyze your current customer base, demographics, and market trends. Don't just go after the dollars, find the client base that you are passionate about serving.

Remember, it's crucial to prioritize long-term success and the well-being of your team over short-term financial gains. Be selective in choosing your clients and avoid entering into compromising situations by not working with people who do not meet your client profile. Have clarity on who you don't want to serve and who you won't work with, and be confident in referring them out to other companies.

In the end, it's the relationships built on trust and integrity that will create a successful business and fulfilling career. Maintain a focus on serving clients who align with your values and vision, and never let desperation cloud your judgment.

CHAPTER 6

STREAMLINING THE CHAIN OF COMMAND

The Squadron Model in real estate management.

In this chapter, we will cover how to create a clear chain of command and the importance of leadership.

As a young pilot-in-training, anticipating my first solo cross-country flight consumed my thoughts. This is a major milestone that requires flying skills and expert airmanship. I dreamed of this moment because it meant my instructor and chief pilot trusted that I was ready to take flight with full responsibility.

After hours of preparation and meticulous planning, I was finally ready to embark on this solo journey.

The night before the flight, I double-checked every detail, from weather forecasts to flight route calculations. As dawn broke, I walked toward the plane with a sense of determination and excitement coursing through my veins. I resolved to prove to myself that I had the discipline and the skill to become a captain one day.

At the airstrip, I diligently completed each item on my pre-flight checklist, speaking the tasks out loud to reinforce my focus. Just as I prepared for takeoff, an unexpected delay occurred. Unfazed, I resumed my routine and was eventually cleared to take off.

The flight itself was a dream come true. My calculations were spot on, the weather remained as predicted, and my landing was smooth and precise. Elated, I strode into the flight deck, expecting a round of applause from my peers and instructors.

Instead, I was met with the stern face of the Chief Pilot, who inquired about my whereabouts. Confused, I stuttered a response, only to learn that they were three minutes away from initiating a search and rescue operation. As it turned out, the delay on the runway had not been reported to the dispatcher, creating a dangerous miscommunication.

That moment, which should have been one of triumph and joy, was a harsh lesson in the importance of the chain of command.

The realization that my negligence could have led to severe consequences down the line was sobering. This experience molded me into a more diligent, conscientious pilot, forever aware of the importance of the chain of command.

In aviation, lives are at stake, but even in less dangerous professions, such as real estate, a lack of communication can lead to financial losses. Because of this, it is important to have a clear chain of command in place for your team, even if you are not the one in charge.

When I started my team in 2012, my goal wasn't to sell thousands of homes, win awards, or become number one. My goal was to build the best real estate team on the planet, and as the team got better, it would allow me to elevate my thoughts and actions. My ultimate goal was independence and freedom to work on what I wanted, when I wanted, and with whom I wanted.

A team leader must carefully consider the composition and roles of team members to ensure that they are well-suited to their assigned tasks and that they work well together. A well-constructed and well-led team will be able to achieve great things.

> **Framework:** Before you grow, create clear roles and re-sponsibilities for each position in the organization. Because people come and go, it is better to create positions that can last forever instead of building them around a specific person. Also, help your team understand the difference between the person and the position. This is important because if you have a certain person in a certain role for a long time, and that person moves to a different position in the organization, other people may still go to them for roles and responsibilities they no longer have. As a leader, be clear with your team about what each role is and who is occupying the position. Be flexible that the person may change but the position remains.

Team leaders must define the lines of authority and communication within the organization and establish a chain of command. The most effective way to do this is what I have come to call the Squadron Model, which limits leadership to seven direct reports.

The Squadron Model ensures that each team member has a defined role and responsibilities within the organization. It helps prevent confusion and conflicting orders by creating a clear hierarchy of authority. Under this model, no more than seven agents should report to a senior agent, no more than seven ISAs should report to the Director of ISA, no more than seven administrators should report to the Director of Operations, no more than seven listing agents should report to a listing coordinator, and so on.

Team leaders need to think about hierarchies as a structure for communication and effectiveness. A lack of clear structure and hierarchies causes many system breakdowns. Emphasizing smaller teams allows for more personalized and individualized attention from the leader, which can help to build stronger relationships and trust among team members. It also allows for more effective communication and decision-making, as the leader is more closely connected to the team's work.

As you grow beyond seven people on your team, the need for structure comes into play. Team leaders must establish senior directors when their team grows beyond fourteen people. I call this building layers of leadership. Any time you have a team member between you and another team member, you have a layer of leadership. That person has clear responsibilities, owns something of importance, and has the authority to make decisions.

Think of it like this: Person B reports to Person A. Person A reports to you. A single layer of leadership.

Imagine a team of forty-nine agents. The squadron model would establish seven squadrons. Each squadron would have a senior agent that would report to the Director of Squadrons. The Director of Squadrons, commonly referred to as a Director of Sales, would no longer have to hold forty-nine agents accountable; they would only need to get reports from seven senior agents. This principle works with all departments, from listings, closings, sales, etc.

Now, imagine a two-hundred-person team. Who reports to the Chief Executive Officer?

The Chief Financial Officer, Chief Operations Officer, Director of Human Resources, Designated Broker, and Director of Sales. By limiting their direct reports, the CEO must delegate authority, responsibility, and leadership to specific positions in the organizational structure.

Establishing a clear chain of command through the Squadron Model is an effective way to manage your real estate team. It ensures that everyone knows their role and responsibilities within the organization and helps to prevent confusion and conflicting orders. It also allows for more personalized and individualized attention from the leader, which can help to build stronger relationships and trust among team members.

Mastery: If your team is missing a clear chain of command, take the time to identify and define each role and reporting structure. It may sound pointless or lacking collaboration, but I believe you will find the opposite to be true. When your team knows their roles and the roles of others, they will have more flexibility and freedom.

The following points will help:

- What is the current structure of your team, and does it have a clear chain of command?
- Do your team members know who to go to when they have certain questions? Do they know which position to go to with specific reports?
- Are there any communication breakdowns or conflicts within the team currently? Align the team to identify com-

munication challenges and remove the noise. Streamline the channels of communication, compile frequently asked questions, and create an easy way to share important knowledge with the entire team.

- How does your team currently handle decision-making and delegation of tasks?

- Are there any current redundancies or inefficiencies in the team's workflow? It's easy to add, add, and add systems. Take the time to identify and report redundancies, allowing you to cut, cut, cut.

- Do all team members have a clear understanding of their roles and responsibilities within the organization? The individual needs to know their role as well as the other team members. Build in a mechanism for team members to cross-train to expand their breadth of knowledge.

- How does your team handle accountability and responsibility for tasks and projects? Do your team members know how to report back?

- How is leadership currently distributed within the team?

$1M: Many leaders have a trust problem. They think nobody can do it better than them and refuse to delegate. Don't be this person.

- Are there any areas where the team could benefit from a more defined structure or hierarchy?

- What steps can you take to start developing a clear chain of command and communication structure for your team?

NEXT STEPS:
HOW TO STREAMLINE YOUR
CHAIN OF COMMAND

- Assess the current structure of your team and identify areas for improvement. Do this by writing down your organization structure, all positions, and the person who occupies that role. You will likely have one person in more than one position.

- Determine the expected growth rate of your team and plan for future expansion. Do this by writing down your organizational structure one, two, and five years from now with assumptions on the production you will have at that time and the positions required to make it happen.

- Evaluate the current communication processes within your team and identify areas for improvement. Identify how communication flows up and down in the organization.

- Develop a clear hierarchy of authority within the team, with defined roles and responsibilities for each member.

- Establish a decision-making process that is effective and efficient for the team. This will evolve as your team evolves.

- Implement a system for accountability and responsibility for tasks and projects.

- Consider using the Squadron Model (or make up your own) as a guide for developing your clear chain of command and communication structure.

- Encourage open communication and collaboration among team members to foster a positive and productive team culture.

- Regularly review and evaluate the effectiveness of your chain of command and make necessary adjustments.
- Invest in leadership development and training to continually improve the effectiveness of your team's leadership structure.

By establishing senior directors when your team grows beyond 14 people, you can delegate authority, responsibility, and leadership to positions. This allows you to establish a clear communication hierarchy to avoid confusion and backlash.

CHAPTER 7

COMPENSATING YOUR SALES TEAM

A guide to paying real estate agents.

In this chapter, we will explore the different methods of commission-based pay and incentives for optimal performance.

As the fifth anniversary of my real estate team approached, I had every reason to celebrate. The team had grown, we had some solid success stories under our belts, and the future looked promising. Yet, there was an unsettling undercurrent that threatened the stability of my team. I had a one-size-fits-all compensation plan, where each agent on the team would split the commission from each sale with the team. This seemingly fair approach had served me well, but cracks were beginning to show because it lacked nuance and opportunity for growth. It also lacked optionality for agents who favor things other than maximizing their split with the brokerage.

Recruiting and retaining agents was becoming increasingly difficult, as many agents were lured away by agencies with more attractive splits. It was a frustrating cycle that seemed to have no end in sight. That was when a dear friend of mine—who happened to run a highly successful eight-figure coaching company—recommended I read Daniel Pink's *Drive*. In this groundbreaking book, Pink suggests that while monetary incentives can increase motivation in the short term, they can be detrimental to motivation in the long run.

This concept struck a chord with me, as I had observed this pattern in my agents' performance. Whenever an agent asked for a raise in commission splits, I would typically oblige when I was scared to lose that agent. The logic seemed sound: the agent would be more motivated to sell more homes, benefiting the company in the long run. However, time and time again, their performance would decline following the raise. In some cases, they actually made less money as a result. I realized this phenomenon wasn't about the money. My agents craved more than just a bigger split.

They wanted independence, freedom, recognition, and security. I needed to find a way to give them what they truly wanted. This realization led me to reevaluate my approach to compensation, and in doing so, I unlocked the true potential of my team.

One of my most exceptional agents, Jane (not her real name), had the skills, knowledge, and performance that would allow her to negotiate a higher split with any broker. But that wasn't what Jane really wanted. She craved security, recognition, and a sense of pride in her work.

Together, Jane and I devised a new compensation plan that catered to her needs. We established a base pay that provided her with the security she sought while also implementing a bonus structure that rewarded her exceptional performance. It was a win-win solution that empowered her to reach new heights in her career.

The key takeaway from this journey was the importance of being creative and open-minded when creating a compensation plan. You might not be able to offer base pay or salary right away, but as you grow you want to be thinking about ways to create win-win compensation plans to keep your cost-of-goods-sold down and retention high.

Long-term relationships can never be solely based on money, as they are unsustainable and ultimately unfulfilling. By taking the time to understand what truly drives each agent on my team, I can provide them with the tools to succeed, and in turn, foster a stronger, more cohesive real estate team that was built to last.

As a real estate team leader, it is important to have a clear and effective method of compensating your agents. The goal is to align incentives to encourage agents to choose to take action and perform. It is possible to have an overly generous compensation structure, just as you can underpay an agent. Either way, their performance will suffer.

I've found that many real estate team leaders lack knowledge of the compensation methods that will most effectively align incentives and performance. The method of pay you choose can impact the motivation and performance of your sales team, and, ultimately, the success of your business. Because of this, it is important to choose a method of payment that aligns with your company's goals and motivates your agents to perform at their best. By understanding the different payment methods, you can make an informed decision that will support the success of your business.

Here are some compensation methods:

Commission-Based Pay: Commission-based pay is the most common method of compensating real estate agents. Agents are paid a percentage of the sale price for each property they sell. This method incentivizes sales and increasing revenue for the company. It is also cost-effective because agents are not paid a fixed salary. Knowing that most agents will accept this plan of payment, your goal is to recruit, recruit, and recruit. With this method, you don't have to pay for labor, only results.

Salary plus Commission: This method of pay combines a fixed salary with a commission. Agents receive a base salary, which provides financial stability, and earn a commission on each sale they make. This payment method is beneficial for agents who are new to the industry and may not have established a sales track record or for those who prefer the security of a fixed salary. Don't underestimate this method of payment.

This can be used as a bonus for attracting quality agents. It is also an excellent method for paying a senior agent who is taking on leadership roles.

> **Mastery:** I've used this method to give myself the freedom to step out of production—instead of referring all of my personal business to another agent, I hired a partner on salary plus commission.

Let's dig into this option a little more. The salary plus commission plan has a break-even point. For example, if you pay a salary of $60,000 per year, or $5,000 a month, how many homes does the agent have to sell for the year to break even? Let's assume each sale is a $10,000 commission check. The salaried agent needs to sell six listings to break even. If my partner sold only six homes in a year, her split is effectively 100%. That is not very good. However, let's imagine she sells thirty-six listings with a gross commission income of $360,000. You paid her $60,000 to make $360,000. That is a 16.6% split of the cost of goods sold.

> **Framework:** This method should only be offered to someone committed. They can't come and go as they please because they are employees and have set hours.

It also is important to give a salary-plus-commission agent a bonus on each sale. Using the example above, consider offering a bonus of 5% of each sale. That would take the effective split from 16.6% to 21.6%. That is a fantastically profitable arrangement.

Bonus: A bonus is a one-time payment awarded to agents for meeting specific performance targets. This method of pay is useful for recognizing and rewarding top-performing agents. The bonus amount can be based on sales volume, performance, or a combination of the two. Remember, incentives drive all behavior. You need a benchmark, target, and carrot for top performers to strive for. Create a win-win benchmark and when they hit the mark, pay them handsomely.

Profit Sharing: In a profit-sharing arrangement, agents receive a portion of the company's profits based on their sales performance. This method of pay aligns the incentives of agents with the success of the company and motivates them to focus on achieving results. Be careful with this method because you open up your books to scrutiny.

> **Framework:** There are a thousand ways to manipulate the books to your advantage. Don't do it! Someone on your team will find it and call you out, ruining your credibility and the intent of profit sharing.

The value of profit sharing is the person will work harder for something they feel they have ownership of. They own part of the profit if the team does well. Don't abuse this.

> **Mastery:** Profit sharing is a great payment method for a chief-level person with major leadership roles.

Stock Options: Stock options allow agents to purchase company stock at a discounted price while working toward the success of the company. This method of payment is a long-term investment for agents and provides a sense of ownership and responsibility in the business. This is an excellent retention method for people you feel your business truly can't live without.

> **Framework:** In my experience, everybody can be replaced if necessary. Don't be held hostage.

Spiffs: These are short-term incentives that are paid to agents for meeting specific sales targets. This method of payment can be used to motivate agents and encourage them to focus on a specific lead or method of selling. Be aware that big mistakes are often made on using spiffs as rewards for contests.

The team leader often sees an increase in activity followed by massive drop-offs. I don't recommend doing spiffs unless you have a lead source you want them to focus on. (I prefer calling these contests because there needs to be an element of fun.) For example, you decide to run a five-star review contest where the winner receives five hundred dollars. Your team gets excited because it's a contest and sees the reward as a fun bonus. They work hard to get as many 5-star reviews as possible. During the terms of the contest, you will see a huge increase in reviews. Once the winner is announced, you will experience a large drop-off. However! Now your team knows how to ask clients to leave a positive review.

Contests are great ways to use spiffs and also improve team connections and bonding.

Allowances: Allowances are payments that are made to agents to cover specific expenses related to their work, such as travel, marketing, or technology. This method of pay helps offset costs and provides additional support to agents.

Draw Against Commission: In a draw against commission arrangement, agents receive a guaranteed income in advance, which is then deducted from their commission earnings. This method of payment can be useful for agents who are new to the industry or who are facing a slow sales period. It provides a steady income while they work to establish themselves.

A method that has served me well is a draw where the new agent receives three monthly commission checks, for example, $2,000 a month for up to three months. Imagine the agent sells their first home and they receive $6,000 after team splits. Because they were already given $6,000 in draws, they receive $0 and are square with the team. This method gives the agent time to build their pipeline of sales during the most critical first 90-day period in their real estate career.

Implementing a compensation plan for your agents can seem overwhelming, especially if you will be changing an already established structure. There will be confrontations and complaints, but rest assured, you will have more complaints, conflicts, and loss of talent for lacking the courage to give clarity on how you compensate your agents.

If you are an agent, how do you feel about your current compensation plan? Do you understand what you get paid and why?

Remember that compensation plans are not written in stone. Like most contracts, you can amend it in the future. Many of the largest tech companies change compensation plans every year to align with their mission and to adapt to the market and their clients. Use compensation to encourage the behavior you want to see.

NEXT STEPS:
HOW TO COMPENSATE
YOUR TEAM LIKE A PRO

- Determine your company's goals and objectives. What kind of performance are you looking to see from your agents?

What is the end goal for your business? If your splits are too generous then you will be providing an incentive for lazy behavior. In my experience, when people reach their comfort income level, they tend to mail it in at work.

- Assess your current compensation structure. What are your current methods of payment? Do you have special deals? Even if you think they are secret, they aren't! Everyone will find out once someone gets a special deal. If you provide an incentive, keep it above board. Make sure your compensation plan is profitable. It is okay for both the team members and the company to make a profit. So, to play the long game, find the profitable position for both parties. Agents will stay at companies with a compensation plan that is fair and profitable for both. Long-time agents know that 100%-split companies and companies with cap rates have issues.

- Read up on different compensation methods and their benefits. When you recruit a new team member, ask them about the compensation plans from their previous agencies. Identify all the hidden fees like desk fees, office fees, E&O fees, tech fees, and more. If the commission split is generous, then the brokers are making it up through creative monetization of the agent's actions.

- Clearly and effectively communicate your compensation plan to your agents. Articulate how the plan allows the team to grow by being profitable long-term and adding security to the employees on the payroll. Share your expenses with the team.

- Regularly review and assess the performance of your agents and adjust your compensation plan to maintain alignment with your company's goals and objectives. You know if your compensation plan is in alignment by observing your agent's behaviors.

With the right steps and mindset, you can create a plan that motivates your team and supports the success of your business. Our compensation plan is in writing and available for everyone to see. We don't make it a secret. Everyone is on the same page and same plan. There is no gameplay or politics on our team.

CHAPTER 8

GEOMETRIC GROWTH

Four strategies for building
faster success.

---

*In this chapter, we will explore four areas
real estate teams can improve to achieve
geometric growth and maximize their potential
for success in the market. The four metrics are:
sell more units, sell higher-priced units, sell
more units per client, and make more per unit.*

In March 2008, I took my first steps into the real estate indus-try. I had saved up a few thousand dollars—the equivalent of a six-month window—to make it work. That was all I had.

My beloved Volvo 850T was sold for $5,500, and in its place, I drove a spray-painted green 1984 Subaru GL wagon that I bought from my father-in-law for a mere $100. The remaining $5,400 was my lifeline to pay bills until my first real estate commission check would hopefully arrive.

Month after month, I hustled and learned everything I could about the industry. And I finally closed my first deal at the end of the sixth month, with just $300 left in my bank account. I was no longer driving the Subaru because I couldn't afford gas to put in the tank, instead, I was using a bus pass to get to the office each day. When I had an appointment, I would borrow my mother-in-law's car. The closing was my second lifeline, but the universe had other plans. In August 2008, the housing market collapsed and our marketplace went silent. Not a single closed sale for five more long months.

The only way to survive this new challenging landscape was to outwork every single agent out there. Ten to twelve-hour days became the norm for me as I tried to build a successful career in the face of adversity. For the next couple of years, I said yes to every opportunity that came my way and out-worked everyone else. Slowly but surely I began to see success.

But this success had a hidden price. The relentless workload took its toll on my health, my relationships, and my spirit.

By my third year in the business, I was barely hanging on and I couldn't remember a single day from that year. I missed important life events and realized that no amount of money was worth this level of exhaustion.

In search of a better way, I joined a mastermind group where I met Jay Abraham, a renowned business guru. Jay taught us how to think critically about our businesses and our actions. He introduced us to the concept of geometric growth versus linear growth, and it changed the trajectory of my career. It is a simple concept, that when you do things by addition like working harder, you get incremental results and added stress. But if you can think in terms of doing a series of things that multiply each other, you gain a geometric advantage. In business, geometric growth is found when you can sell more things at higher prices to more people and the same people more often.

In this chapter, I will share the invaluable lessons I learned from Jay, as well as my personal journey of becoming a million-dollar real estate agent. It's a story of resilience, determination, and finding the right balance between hard work and working smart. It's a testament to the power of the human spirit, and the knowledge that no matter the challenges, with the right mindset, tools, and perseverance, success is within your reach.

If you were only to increase one of these metrics, you would see incremental growth and likely struggle as the law of diminishing returns sets in. To overcome this law, you need to obtain increases in all four areas to experience massive growth.

It's time to stop thinking of incremental growth and start thinking of exponential growth. This change in mindset is the key to real estate team success.

> **$1M:** A 10% increase in all four areas is not a 40% increase; it can add 2X, 3X, or 10X to your bottom line.

This type of growth, also known as geometric growth, can be achieved through smart sales and marketing strategies.

Sell more units: This is the most obvious metric that all teams are fighting to increase. Increasing sales requires more agents, expanding your target market, increasing marketing efforts, and streamlining the sales process to minimize loss and increase conversions. To sell more units, have your team work to turn every listing into another listing.

- To do this it is more important to promote your new listings to other owners than it is to find buyers.
- Use this promotion as a job interview for your next listing.
- Target buyers who have properties to sell. You can use a call to action like, "If you buy this home, I will sell yours for top dollar." Get your seller to agree to look at contingent-on-sale-of-home offers and proactively promote that in your marketing. "This owner is accepting offers subject to your home selling. Call now for details." Or, "Do you have a home to sell before you can buy? No problem, trade your home for this one."

Sell higher-priced units: Targeting a more affluent clientele, offering high-end properties, and providing unique value propositions can help real estate teams sell higher-priced units. Have a strategy to help current owners remodel or improve their homes. If you can improve someone's property by 10%, you will have an impact on your revenues and your client's results. Many marketing efforts are the same cost-per-unit, and knowing this should encourage you to target areas and clients with the highest price points.

Sell more units per client: It is far more expensive to acquire a new client than to keep a current one. Focus on selling buyers more than one home. Start an investor seminar strategy. Start a vacation rental funnel. Follow up with clients to see if they want to upsize or downsize. There are endless ways to ethically sell more units to one client. Focus on building strong relationships, offering complementary services, and providing excellent customer service to your current clients.

Make more per unit: Having a fee strategy and being paid by commission-only is another way to achieve geometric growth. The commission is the largest cost-of-sale for a homeowner. What you may not realize is they are often willing to pay for added services, but if you don't offer any, you are missing out. Think about staging fees, advanced marketing fees, transaction management fees, early termination fees, a fee you charge when they get a discount on commission (for example 5% with a $997 marketing fee), and video tour fees. There are thousands of services you can offer a buyer or seller, and doing so will set your agency apart from everyone else and improve customer satisfaction.

By focusing on these four strategies, real estate teams can achieve significant geometric growth and maximize their potential for success in the market. Whether you are looking to sell more units, sell higher-priced units, sell more units per client, or make more per-unit transactions, these strategies can help you reach your goals and grow your business.

NEXT STEPS:
HOW TO ACHIEVE GEOMETRIC GROWTH

- Change your business mindset. Not all clients are worth the same to your company. That may sound harsh and doesn't sound fair, but it's true. And early in your development you likely can't say no, but as you grow, you need to target higher price points, higher compensation, most-likely-to-transaction leads. You can target neighborhoods with higher sales prices and you can add more value to charge higher commissions.

- Identify ways to increase sales, such as hiring more agents, expanding the target market, increasing marketing efforts, and working with clients who buy and sell more than one unit per year—builders, investors, and the land marketplace.

- Sell higher-priced units. Target a more affluent clientele, offer high-end properties, and provide unique value propositions. Also, consider offering services that help owners improve their homes prior to listing or after purchasing. If you helped every seller increase their value by 5%, you increased your income by 5%. You can give yourself a raise immediately and make more money for your clients.

- Build strong relationships with your clients by staying in touch with them after the sale. Make that contact consistent. Approximately 90% of buyers and sellers never hear from their agent after closing. By staying in touch with your past clients you can offer complementary services and provide expert advice moving forward. These clients are far more likely to use you again and refer you to people they know. This will lead to you creating a referral strategy that will include a VIP client program. Encourage repeat business by educating your clients and team members on investing in real estate. Start a property management company to service your investor's portfolios.

- Develop a fee strategy and consider offering additional services for a fee. Look for ways to charge for added value, such as staging, advanced marketing, transaction management, early termination, and video tour fees. Bundle them up and charge more. Don't be like everyone else in the market. Charge more and be the premium service provider. You have the decision to make; you either discount your fees or find ways to win by being more efficient than the competition. When you charge the most, you gain a huge advantage psychologically with the consumer; the thing, product, or service that costs the most has the perceived value of being the best and highest quality. Anyone can sell a home; it takes luxury service to give an experience worth paying for. Nobody comes to our company thinking we are the cheapest. They come knowing we are the best.

By following these steps, your real estate team can achieve geometric growth and maximize your potential for success in the market.

CHAPTER 9

FEE STRUCTURES

Maximizing revenue per transaction in real estate.

In this chapter, we will focus on fee structures for maximizing revenue per transaction in real estate.

---

can still remember the day as if it were yesterday; the day I sold the biggest commercial lot of my career. The property was worth several million, and I had the good fortune to represent both the buyer and the seller, netting my team the entire commission. The transaction was, and still is, the largest commission I had ever made.

But even that incredible commission pales compared to the lesson I learned from the seller during that process, a lesson that has helped me generate untold millions and forever changed how I approach my work.

I'll never forget the first meeting with my soon-to-be client. A towering figure, he had been responsible for developing hundreds of Sears Roebuck stores across North America during the 1970s. Sears in the '70s was what Amazon is in the 2020s.

When he and his wife were scouting locations for new stores in my hometown via helicopter, his wife fell in love with the view. He promptly bought the land, leveled it, and built a 10,000-square-foot home for them to live in. And now, he was sitting in my office, looking to sell a commercial lot he owned.

It was during this meeting that he imparted the wisdom that has since shaped my entire approach to business. With an intense gaze, he said, "Nick, remember this one thing, no matter what anyone ever tells you, no matter what your competition will say, no matter what your competition charges, there is no such thing as an unreasonable amount of profit."

He was a true capitalist, and he was absolutely right. From that moment on, I focused on raising prices as long as I could raise the value beyond what someone was willing to pay. My new mantra became: *always deliver more value than the price, but never lower prices because I lack the creativity to add value.*

His lesson, so succinctly delivered that day in my office, has proven to be invaluable. It has allowed me to grow both personally and professionally, continuously pushing the boundaries of what I thought was possible.

As I reflect on that meeting nearly a decade later, I am grateful for the wisdom he shared and the impact it has had on my career. Fee maximization is an art, and his lesson taught me to pursue it without fear or hesitation. By embracing the idea that there is no such thing as an unreasonable amount of profit, I have been able to unlock success beyond my wildest dreams.

Let's look at some ways to do this in real estate.

As we discussed in Chapter 8, it's important to have a comprehensive fee structure to maximize revenue per transaction. The commission is, and likely always will be, the biggest line item for sellers, buyers, and agents. It is also the one line item that will garner the most attention. In my experience, fees tied to services and value are rarely met with resistance as long as they are presented upfront and honestly.

Here are ten fee structures to implement into your business model:

- **Listing Transaction Fee:** Paid by the seller for closing coordination and execution. A listing transaction fee can be charged to the seller at closing and ranges from $250 to $1,997. This fee can help increase revenue per transaction and provide value to the seller by helping to cover the cost of listing coordination.

- **Buyer Transaction Fee:** Paid by the buyer for closing coordination and execution. A buyer transaction fee can be charged to the buyer at closing and ranges from $250 to $1,997. I once charged an investor $2,997 without any pushback.

- **Early Termination Fee:** Paid by the seller. An early termination fee can be charged to the seller if they cancel a listing within a certain timeframe. For example, if the seller cancels within the first thirty days, they agree to pay a marketing fee of $2,497. This fee can help mitigate the impact of early cancellations and increase revenue for the real estate team.

- **Commission Strategy:** Paid by the listing agent. By offering less than the total commission to the buyer's agent and charging more on the listing side, real estate teams can increase their revenue per transaction. The buyer's agent commission should be based on the market rate, and there is no need to pay more than necessary. This one shift can increase listing revenues by over 40%.

- **Transaction Fee:** Paid by the agent to the team.. A transaction fee can be taken from the commission at closing and ranges from $150 to $1,000. This fee can help cover the cost of transaction coordination. Most teams and brokers hire a dedicated closing coordinator to assist the agent during the closing process. In return, the agent agrees to this transaction fee. It is best for the team or brokerage to make this a standard transaction fee instead of an optional fee. If it is optional, you will not get a buy, and the service will be abused.

- **Error and Omission (E&O) Fee:** Paid monthly by your agents. An E&O fee is a monthly fee that is accrued and collected through the commission disbursement. This fee should range from $20 to $40 a month and can help cover the cost of E&O insurance.

Framework: Each team or brokerage should carry an insurance policy that protects agents from liability for making an E&O. The policy also opens up opportunities for the agent to explore, like working for banks, completing BPO Broker Price Opinions, relocation companies, and asset management companies. Many teams take their total premium and times it by two to arrive at a yearly amount. This amount is then divided by the total number of agents to arrive at an annual fee per agent. The agent is then charged per month.

- **Technology Fee:** Paid monthly by your agent. A technology fee can be accrued and collected through the commission disbursement to the agent. This fee ranges from $20 to $200 a month and can help cover the cost of the team's technology stack.

- **Team Member Benefits Package:** Paid monthly by your agent. A Team Member Benefits Package can be offered and includes all services from office space, supplies, tech stack, E&O, and more. This fee ranges from $50 to $500 a month and can be collected through the commission disbursement.

- **Commission Advance Fee:** Paid by your agent. By providing agents an advance on future closings, real estate teams can collect a fee of $100 to $500, depending on the commission size.

- **Less than X% Commission Fee:** Paid by the seller when signing the listing. If a client wants a commission that is less than the average commission, a fee can be charged to cover upfront marketing costs. This fee ranges from $497 to $1,997 and can be collected any time the commission is less than the average. For example, let's say my average commission is 6%. The seller negotiates 5% saving an entire 1% of the sales price commission and agrees to pay $997 upfront for marketing fees and photos. Sellers love this alternative to paying a full-price commission. Many sellers just want a deal, which allows you to budge on commission and at the same time cover your upfront expenses.

NEXT STEPS:
HOW TO IMPROVE YOUR FEE STRUCTURE

- Review the current fee structure for your real estate team and identify any areas that can be improved. Most teams don't charge for their services beyond commission.

This is outdated. The consumer expects to pay for service, and when you don't charge for added value, you diminish your value.

- Consider how your team can provide value to clients and agents through the new fee structure. The structure should be attractive to the client and to the team member who is selling it. Agents will love ways to make more money. Your clients will love the valuable services.

- The next step is to develop a clear and concise policy. This policy should outline the fees associated with different services and be easy to understand. What is the promise, what is the payoff, and how much does it cost?

- It is important to train team members on the new fee structure so that they can communicate the changes to clients and agents effectively. This will help ensure that everyone is on the same page and that the structure is implemented smoothly. Your team will hesitate, and there will be resistance at first, so it's important to acknowledge that change can be hard. A new agent/team member won't know any difference and will understand the fees immediately, but be sure to acknowledge your long-time agents and praise them for making the changes.

- Once the fee structure has been developed and the team has been trained, it is time to communicate the changes to clients and agents. This can be done through various channels, including email, newsletters, and face-to-face meetings.

- Regularly monitor the effectiveness of the new structure and make any necessary adjustments. This will help to ensure that it continues to meet the needs of clients and agents, and remains competitive and compliant. You can't expect to be amazing at selling a new product or service in the beginning; it takes practice and refinement.

- There is the carrot and there is the stick. If agents are not offering the company fee structures to their client—like the client-paid transaction fee—then charge the agent for not asking.

> **$1M:** If you don't have a consequence, agents won't ask because most people do everything they can to avoid confrontation. The simple truth is that clients also don't like confrontation and will accept fees, especially when they are tied to value and service.

By implementing these steps, real estate teams can maximize revenue per transaction and provide value to their clients and agents.

CHAPTER 10

MINIMIZING RISK

Using proven marketing risk reversals to improve client relations.

In this chapter, we will discuss how you can eliminate client risk and guarantee satisfaction with proven marketing strategies.

I n the year 2008, life threw me an unexpected curveball. Focus Air Cargo, the airline I worked for, announced they were shutting down.

Feeling disoriented during a layover in Bangkok, Thailand, I signed up for an online real estate course. Little did I know, I would spend nine days in a hotel room battling the flu, an ear infection, and an eye infection. During that time, I completed all 90 hours of the coursework, took the exam, and returned home as a newly licensed real estate agent.

This career shift wasn't a random decision; I wanted to start a family, be a devoted father and husband, and live a life closer to home. However, as I embarked on my new journey, the real estate market took a nosedive. The housing market collapse in 2008 was catastrophic, and millions of Americans faced foreclosure, short sales, and bankruptcy.

During this tumultuous time, I worked for banks in their Real Estate Owned (REO) department. This role was emotionally taxing, as I had to knock on doors and inform people that they no longer owned their homes. Witnessing this firsthand taught me much about human nature and the power of fear.

I noticed that many of these homeowners never tried to sell their homes; they never reached out for help. The primary reason? Fear. They were paralyzed by the risks and the uncertainty, so they did nothing. That's when it hit me—what if people had the confidence to act? How many more would take the leap to sell their homes if they knew I could remove their risks and in turn increase their confidence?

The concept of risk reversal quickly became a guiding principle. I understood that people are more motivated by pain than pleasure and that selling the upside is limiting and very competitive because every agent in town uses the upside as their selling proposition. To truly help people and increase sales in real estate, I had to find ways to reduce their pain and remove uncertainty. This chapter will explore how risk reversal strategies can transform your real estate business and motivate clients to work with you.

As a successful real estate team leader, I've learned the importance of taking calculated risks to stand out from the competition and attract more clients. I also understand the power of minimizing risk for my clients to ensure their satisfaction and increase conversions. That's why I have spent a lot of time mastering the art of risk reversals. This technique eliminates the risk for the client and puts them at ease when considering working with my team. It takes a lot of studies to master this information. In the following pages, I will do my best to give you a simplified version of these complex concepts.

Below are 15 proven marketing risk reversals that have helped me elevate my real estate business. Don't think you have to try all of these. It's ok to pick one or two and just do those.

- **Money-Back Guarantee:** The most powerful sales proposition for an agent is we don't get paid if we don't sell. By offering a money-back guarantee, you remove risk from the client's decision to work with your team. When everyone does something in an industry, everyone stops selling it!

One of the most powerful selling propositions in the real estate industry is that we get paid on contingency. This means that we pay for advertising, labor, expenses, provide advice and risk it all by betting that we will be the agent that sells the home and receives the commission. We go all in on the fact that we don't get paid unless something closes.

> **Mastery:** The majority of agents don't sell the value of the lockbox. I will sell the lockbox based on what it does for the client. It keeps their home secure and only licensed agents can access it. Having a lockbox also helps me because it notifies me of all showings so that I can get feedback from the showing agent. I know most other agents won't even mention the lockbox and I sell it as a value.

- **Trial Period:** Allowing clients to try my services before committing to a long-term relationship eliminates the risk of dissatisfaction. Consider offering thirty and sixty-day listing trials. I have even done complimentary one-day listings with great success. At the end of the one-day listing, I call the client and explain how the one-day is up and I will honor the agreement or we can extend for thirty, sixty, or one-hundred-eighty days. By this point, I have demonstrated a huge amount of value in that one day and they would never consider going through the hassle, inconvenience, and unknown of signing up with another agent.

- **Satisfaction Guarantee:** A satisfaction guarantee gives clients peace of mind knowing they can fire me and terminate the agreement if they're not happy with my services. Offering your clients this guarantee allows them to cancel anytime if they are unsatisfied. Establish a satisfaction guarantee with an easy exit because most people will hire you for being upfront and honest. If you are competing with another agent, and you have this policy and the other agent doesn't, you will win the listing even if you charge more money.

> **$1M:** The truth is, if your client is unhappy and has decided to cancel, there is little you can do to stop them. You can use the agreement as a legal block to the cancellation request but be warned, you are creating a battle. Your only hope is to diffuse the situation, take responsibility, and ask for a second chance even if the reason they are upset is not your fault.

- **No-Questions-Asked Return Policy:** This policy makes it easy for clients to cancel your service without jumping through hoops. Don't make the cancellation process tough and be upfront about how easy it will be. The primary objective of satisfaction guarantees and easy return policies is to leave unhappy customers with nothing to complain about. If you make it difficult for them to walk away when they want to, they will never stop talking about it. This can tank future sales.

- **No-Commitment:** A no-commitment, or cancel at any time, offer takes the pressure off the client if they decide to continue working with me. No-commitment language is fantastic and should be found on your website, lead forms, phone scripts, and initial showing appointments with buyers. This differs from the satisfaction guarantee because the satisfaction is once they sign up and list their home with you. No-commitment is meant to lower the sales skepticism allowing the client to cancel an appointment and have the confidence knowing they are not being obligated to sign anything or pay anything for upfront consultations. Let's say I set a listing appointment to tour your house, I will let you know I'm coming over prepared to list if you are ready and believe I'm the right person for the job. However, there is no obligation or pressure to sign. You can also cancel the appointment or agreement if you decide to sign and change your mind.

WAYS TO REASSURE CLIENTS

- **Warranty or Service Contract:** A warranty or service contract eliminates the homeowner's risk of paying for repairs or replacements down the line. Offering a home warranty and pre-inspection to buyers or sellers helps remove the risk of unknown future problems.
- **Best-Price Guarantee:** By offering the best price guarantee, clients know they're getting the best value for their money. Homeowners don't want to overpay and they don't want to underprice their homes. Have you ever lost

a listing because another agent said they could sell it for more? Let's dive in deeper. You go on a listing appointment and give your home-value recommendation. The seller says they want to think about or compare it to another agent. You will say, "My price is based on historical data I am confident in. I also know any agent can say any price. In the unlikely event an agent says they can sell your property for more, call me and run that number by me. I will verify the accuracy of their price and give you a price-match guarantee or be upfront and honest that I can't sell it for that price. Does that sound fair?" This isn't an offer you promote because you will lose credibility in your opinion of value. It is a risk reversal when you know other agents will blow pink smoke to try to buy the listing with a higher list price only to ask for a price reduction in the future.

> **Framework:** Don't be the person who blows smoke at your clients in order to get them to sign with you. If you are, you will lose credibility and won't be able to carry quality agents and clients in the long run.

- **Referral or Testimonial Guarantee:** A referral or testimonial guarantee gives potential clients the assurance that others have had positive experiences working with me. Social proof, reviews, and references are incredibly powerful because they remove uncertainty. Potential clients are more likely to consider your reviews as proof of your quality over your claims about yourself.

- **No-Risk or Low-Risk Investment Option:** This option eliminates the fear of losing money for clients who are hesitant to invest. Homeowners are scared they will spend money to improve their houses and they won't sell. Buyers are worried they will go under contract, not get approved for the loan, and lose money on the inspection and appraisal. With a no-risk program, I can offer a buyer an earnest money guarantee—they can go under contract on a home and if they decide to back out for any reason and the seller doesn't release their earnest money—I will reimburse the buyer. I can lower their risk by agreeing to reimburse them for the home inspection if they don't get approved by the lender. I can offer a no-risk-improvement option to a seller to list their home. I can say the home will sell for $400,000 if you put new carpet in the house and get it professionally cleaned. If the home sells for under $400,000, I will lower my commission to cover the cost of the carpet and cleaning. Of course, the risk is that you may end up having to pay for any of these items, but if you know your market, understand earnest-money contracts, and utilize the expertise of others around you, you are not likely to ever have to pay for any of these options.

WAYS TO REDUCE CLIENT UNCERTAINTY

- **No-Obligation Consultation or Estimate:** A no-obligation consultation or estimate takes the pressure off the client to make a decision. This is the classic free Comparative Market Analysis (CMA).

> **$1M:** Don't use the word FREE; it diminishes the value of the CMA analysis. Instead, call the CMA a property equity report with no cost or obligation.

- **No-Risk Special Offer:** A no-risk or no-brainer special offer allows potential clients to remove risk from consideration. This mindset makes it easier for clients to sign on to the listing program. This is also another way to package any one of the risk reversals and guarantees I have already outlined—as no-risk offers.

- **Risk-Free Trial Membership:** A risk-free or no-risk trial membership allows clients to try my services without any commitment. It's like a free trial, just in a new package. This is best suited for buyers searching your website and is highlighted when they are asked to register.

> **Framework:** You should ask potential buyers to register when they browse your site. This is cheap lead sourcing. Just make sure you follow up on these quickly.

- **No-Risk Evaluation:** A no-risk evaluation, or no-cost assessment, allows clients to assess their home value without any obligation to list their home. This is superior to the classic free CMA offer provided by most real estate agents because when you use the word free, that tells your customer it has no value. Then your customer thinks, "What's the catch?" Now you are in trouble because your client believes what you are offering is a bait and switch to pressure them into a listing or buying a home. You can also offer a buyer a no-cost assessment to determine their buying power.

- **No-Risk Consultation:** A no-risk consultation, or no-cost advice, eliminates the fear of having to pay for advice that may not be useful. This offer would include a custom game plan or roadmap for a specific situation. This language appeals greatly in divorce situations and estate planning because the sellers don't know if they want to list or sell, but require a valuation report. A variation of this service is to offer a fee, and then waive the fee if they decide to list with your company.

> **Framework:** As a lead strategy, reach out to law firms that handle divorce and estate planning and offer a no-cost assessment for their clients. You would be surprised how many clients in these scenarios are calling appraisers.

- **A No-Risk Demonstration Service:** A no-risk demonstration, or no-cost sample, allows clients to try the product or service before committing to it. When working with a buyer, you can write a hypothetical offer on a home they like. This allows them to get familiar with the process and they will be pros when it comes time to write an actual offer. Likewise, you can also show a potential seller the listing paperwork and all the disclosures. Remind them this is just a sample and there is no pressure to sign.

This builds confidence and answers questions they didn't know they had. As the agent, it is your job to build rapport and uncover hidden objections.

By using these risk reversals, I've been able to increase conversions in my real estate business.

NEXT STEPS:
HOW TO MINIMIZE RISK

- Have you worked with a real estate agent before? If so, what was your experience like?
- What concerns do you have about working with a real estate agent?
- Are you worried about losing money in the process of buying or selling a home?
- What would help you feel more confident about making a decision to work with our team?
- Do you have any hesitations about committing to a long-term relationship with an agent?
- What would make you feel more comfortable about trying out our extra services?
- Have you received a property equity report or home analysis before? If not, would you like one?
- Are you worried about paying for advice or services that may not be useful to you?
- Have you considered a home warranty or pre-inspection?
- Would you like to see a demonstration of the offer writing process or receive a custom game plan for your specific situation?

The above questions should have given you insight into which risk reversals are valuable for your marketplace. As you read through them, you probably came up with questions of your own (or edited mine). If you found some questions that work, let me know! I would love to learn from your experience as well.

Step up your real estate game and give clients the peace of mind they deserve by using one or two of these 15 proven marketing risk reversals. From money-back guarantees to no-obligation consultations, these tactics will help you stand out from the competition and secure more conversions. Once you find a winner, go big and market it far and wide.

Say goodbye to uncertainty and hello to happy clients. It's time to elevate your business today!

CHAPTER 11

UNIQUE SELLING PROPOSITION

A guide for real estate team leaders.

In this chapter, we will discuss how to find your team's strengths and differentiating factors to create a winning Unique Selling Proposition (USP).

I remember the day I decided to leave my job as an airline pilot. I had seniority number 33 at a start-up airline, and despite my knowledge, skills, and abilities, I could not progress. As long as the company grew, I had to wait my turn. If I chose to go to another company no matter my experience level, I had to start at the bottom and wait my turn based on my seniority number. This realization made my stomach drop.

The thought of feeling stuck terrified me, and I was reluctant to seek other opportunities for fear of losing my beloved seniority number. Luckily, I never had to live that life, as I explained earlier. I found my calling in entrepreneurship and real estate, where the better I got, the more I could make and the further I could progress. No seniority numbers were holding me back here.

That doesn't mean people won't try to place limitations on you. One such limitation is the pressure to fit in and comply with the status quo.

During my new-agent orientation class, I remember an established agent telling us everything we couldn't do. "Don't work with anyone beyond your expertise. Don't work outside your marketplace. Don't try selling anything you don't know about." All I heard was, "Stay in your lane and pay your dues." It felt like an attempt to impose an invisible seniority number on us, to keep us from reaching our full potential.

It was the same thing I heard from old-school pilots telling me why the seniority system worked.

But I knew that the key to success in business was to stand out, be unique, and be bold. The more I embraced that mindset, the more eyeballs and attention my team and I attracted.

I recall the day when a potential client walked into my office, fresh from a meeting with our most significant competitor. "I just left your competition, the one that's been in business for 30 years, and everyone uses them," he said. "But while I was there, they kept mentioning you guys. I could tell they were scared. So I came right here because you're obviously different, new, and changing the game. I want to work with you."

That encounter solidified my belief in always striving to offer unique services, narratives, headlines, strategies, and technology systems to the marketplace. It proved to me that breaking free from the chains of seniority and conventional thinking was the right path, and it allowed me to grow and progress in ways I could never have imagined while stuck in my pilot's seat.

In the end, I embraced the challenge of standing out and climbing the ladder of success in real estate. I refused to be confined by the status quo or the establishment, and I encouraged my team to do the same. We rose above the constraints of an invisible seniority number, finding success and fulfillment beyond our wildest dreams.

Unique Selling Propositions (USPs) are essential for real estate teams looking to stand out in a competitive market. When I started my real estate team in 2012, we were the only real estate team in our marketplace. Our USP is the coordinating efforts of a group of people working toward a common goal (Teamwork). While that is still our cornerstone USP, the concept doesn't tell the seller or buyer what's in it for them. That is why you have to develop USPs that purely benefit your clients. The team USP supports your other USPs, but your client needs to see something that works for them as well.

> **Framework:** Over the years, we had to evolve our USPs to stay ahead of the competition and be compelling to the community by giving them what they want in a unique way to make our team stand out.

There are millions of agents, and the consumer sees real estate services as a means to an end. Your goal is to stand out as unique and hyper-valuable. Fortune favors bold marketers.

A USP is a clear, concise statement that outlines what sets your team apart from others in the industry. Let's explore various ways that you can create a winning USP for your team.

- **Know Your Target Audience:** The first step in creating a USP is understanding your target audience. We discussed this in Chapter 5. Who are your ideal clients, and what do they need from a real estate team? This information will help you tailor your USPs to meet their specific needs. Find their root problems and offer a solution. If homes are not selling, we offer our Guarantee Sale Program, where if we don't sell your home in a certain timeframe, we buy it.

- **Identify Your Team's Strengths:** The next step is to identify your team's strengths and what sets you apart from competitors. This could be anything from a unique approach to the home-buying process, a deep understanding of the local market, or exceptional customer service. By focusing on your strengths, you can create a USP that resonates with your target audience and sets your team up for success.

> **Mastery:** Brand your property-buying process as a system, such as our Buyer's Advantage Program or Unique Selling System.

- **Be Specific:** Once you've identified your team's strengths, it's important to be specific about how you deliver value to clients. For example, instead of simply saying that you offer excellent customer service, you could say that you provide 24/7 availability and a dedicated account manager for each client. By being specific, you can clearly communicate the value that your team provides to clients. We've offered free moving services, earnest money protection, guaranteed sales, instant offers, weekend-showing services, dedicated real estate professionals, expert or advanced marketing services, and more.

- **Communicate Consistently:** Once you've created your USP, it's important to communicate it consistently across all of your marketing and sales materials. This includes your website, business cards, flyers, and email signature. By communicating your USP consistently, you can build brand recognition and ensure that your message resonates with potential clients. You will be known for your specific USPs. But keep in mind, it is why people will call you but not why they will sign with you.

- **Offer Guarantees:** Another way to make your USP stand out is by offering guarantees. A guarantee provides clients with peace of mind and shows that you stand behind your services. For example, you could offer a satisfaction guarantee, a no-hassle return policy, or a promise to sell a client's home within a certain timeframe. By offering guarantees, you can differentiate your team and build trust with potential clients. Adding specific timeframes increases response rates. For example, instead of a your-home-sold guarantee, you could have a 59-day home-sale guarantee. Instead of an instant offer, you could have an instant offer within 72 hours of reaching out.

- **Package Multiple Services:** Another way to create a Unique Selling Proposition is to package multiple services into one offering. This allows you to offer a comprehensive solution to your client's needs rather than just one isolated service. By bundling services, you can streamline the process for clients and provide added value. Considering your market has many agents, and someone offers nearly everything, you can be unique by packaging services and giving it a brand name.

- **Focus on Experience:** Another approach to creating a Unique Selling Proposition is to focus on the experience you provide clients. For example, if your team specializes in luxury real estate, you could position your USP around exceptional service and hospitality, similar to a five-star hotel like the Four Seasons. By offering a high level of personalized attention, expert knowledge, and exceptional service, you can create a differentiated experience for your clients.

A Unique Selling Proposition is a vital component of your real estate team's success. By understanding your target audience, identifying your team's strengths, being specific, communicating consistently, and offering guarantees, you can create a winning USP that sets your team apart from the competition and helps you succeed in the competitive world of real estate.

Keep in mind that having a USP isn't the end of it. You have to implement it and run it effectively. I have learned this lesson several times. Here are some common USP pitfalls you can avoid:

- **Failing to Conduct Market Research:** One of the biggest mistakes businesses make with their USP is failing to conduct market research to understand their target audience and what that audience is looking for. Without this information, it's difficult to create a USP that resonates with your target market and sets you apart from the competition.
- **Being Too Vague:** Another common mistake is being too vague when describing your USP. Be specific about what makes your customer service unique and what value it provides to customers.

- **Copying Competitors:** Don't copy your competitors' USPs. This not only lacks originality, but it also makes it difficult to differentiate yourself from others in the market.
- **Not Aligning USP with Business Goals:** Misalignment of your USP and your business goals will lead to havoc in your business. For example, if your goal is to be the low-cost provider, but your USP is around premium service, the two will be in conflict.
- **Failing to Communicate USP Consistently:** Finally, failing to communicate your USP consistently across all marketing and sales materials is a serious mistake. Your USP should be communicated in a consistent manner across all channels to make sure that your message resonates with your target audience. Your team must be well-versed on all your USPs and marketing messages. You need to install your USP in your phone scripts, and emails, not just your marketing efforts.

By avoiding these mistakes and developing a well-thought-out, targeted USP, you can set your business apart from the competition and achieve greater success in the marketplace.

Here are examples of Unique Selling Propositions:
- Certified pre-owned listing
- Guaranteed sale program or we buy it
- Hassle-free listing where if the seller finds the buyer, there is a 0% commission
- Cancellation guarantee
- Coming soon listing programs

- Instant offer program
- Rent-back program
- Buyer-advantage program to off-market or immediate-release notifications.
- Be creative and be specific.

NEXT STEPS:
HOW TO DEVELOP A STRONG USP

- Understand your target market. Identify target customers' needs, preferences, and pain points. Your USP needs to solve people's problems, remove fears and anxieties, and reduce client overwhelm.
- Study your competitors and identify their strengths and weaknesses. Look through their websites and marketing materials to identify gaps in their offerings that your business can fill. If an agent or team has a USP you want, you can find a way to make it your own. While it is always good to be first, sometimes you can be last and outperform everyone else with position and marketing.
- Identify your unique strengths. What key features make your service different from others in the market? The top features are typically guarantees, staging, home warranties, certification process, rent backs, flexible terms, buybacks, adjustable fees, and convenience packages. Never underestimate the power of offering done-for-you service. People will always pay more and pick companies with the most convenient service packages. Remove hassle, and you will increase your strength in the marketplace.

- Develop customer-centric USPs that focus on the benefits your product or service provides to your target customers. Avoid generic statements and emphasize the unique value your business delivers—*full-service listing* is vague and does not differentiate you from the competition. If you are confused you will lose so, be specific.

> **Mastery:** You will likely need more than one USP, our team has dozens because we would rather be specific than vague. And having multiple programs allows you to run multiple ad campaigns throughout the year and avoid ad fatigue.

- Test your USPs with your target audience to ensure they resonate with them. Gather feedback and be open to making adjustments if necessary. Insert the USP in your e-mail campaigns, radio ads, social media posts, and phone scripts. Call past clients and ask them if this new program would have had an impact on their decision to work with you. Call people who went with another company to list or buy their home and see if this program would have moved the needle.

- Use your USPs consistently across all of your marketing channels, including your website, social media, advertising, and sales presentations.

- Implement training to ensure that your team members understand your USPs and can effectively communicate them to customers. This will help create a consistent brand experience and foster customer loyalty.

If you are tired of blending in with the countless other real estate teams in the industry, you need to create a winning USP. It's time to take action and create a USP that will differentiate your real estate team and lead to greater success in the marketplace. Start now! Be bold! Repeat your USP over and over again until the marketplace knows your USP by heart.

CHAPTER 12

WINNING THE LISTING

A step-by-step guide to the listing sales process.

In this chapter, we will discuss how you can achieve results with a streamlined listing process.

As an airline pilot, I was accustomed to precision, order, and regulations. The industry I worked in was one of the most regulated in the world and for a good reason. Flying a giant metal tube at 500 mph, 35,000 feet in the air with 200 souls on board demanded extraordinary attention to detail.

Every flight required painstaking accuracy. From a flight plan with each waypoint perfectly placed in the GPS down to the millimeter to checkpoints, redundancies, and perfect performance measurements. Every action needed to be calculated and done in the right order. A single mistake, error, omission, or deviation from the procedure could result in catastrophe. But the results spoke for themselves: thousands of successful flights daily, all due to the rigorous processes in place.

When I began my real estate career. I was immediately shocked by the lack of procedures and processes in this new world. My first broker had no written process for securing a listing and success seemed to hinge entirely on personality, who you knew, and sheer luck.

I wondered if I applied the same discipline and rigor I had used as a pilot, whether I could create a repeatable process that would improve my listing conversion rate and challenge the complacency of the old guard. So, I got to work developing a systematic approach to real estate that mirrored my experience in the airline industry.

I was winning, not because of my experience, knowledge, and skills, I was winning because the competition had no formal process and were making mistakes.

By my fourth year, my listing process had propelled me to become the number one listing agent in my MLS. My meticulous, structured approach had paid off in spades, and I knew I could scale this success by teaching others to do the same.

As I started building my team, I focused on passing along the listing process I had created. To my delight, new agents were able to learn the process quickly, allowing them to replicate my success in the field. My team thrived, and I couldn't have been prouder.

As a successful real estate agent, I know that the key to success is to have a well-designed and efficient process for generating listing leads, converting them into listings, and successfully closing the sale. Whether you are an established team or just starting as an agent, having a streamlined listing process can make all the difference in your success.

I've gone on more than 3,000 listing appointments and here are some things I have learned:

- Your team must be well-trained and standardized in their approach to listing properties. The listing process is boring to me because I've completed it thousands of times, but that doesn't matter. What matters is that I follow the process because the client has never experienced my listing process before. When I execute it well, I'm looking for the yes and the wow reactions.

- After training thousands of agents on my listing process, I can confidently say it takes fifty real appointments before you start to get good at it. Here is the good news, you don't have to wait that long because once you know the process, you will be better than 95% of all the other agents. They lack a process and will look disorganized and unprofessional compared to you.

- Too much emphasis is placed on buyer-lead conversion because the lead-generating platforms sell buyer leads. That creates a recency bias, meaning that every day you are distracted by buyer leads. Because team leaders spend money on buyer leads, they often take their eyes away from the most profitable and critical part of the real estate business: Getting the listing.

To emphasize this last point, listings are 75% of your profit. Listings will likely be 50% of your sales but two-thirds or more of your profit. There have been years where we sold fewer listings than buyer sides; however, 80% of our profit still came from the listings. Our best revenue and profitable years undoubtedly are when we sign more listing agreements. As a rule of thumb, every listing you sign and properly market is worth two closings. So, if my goal is to sell twenty-four properties or four hundred properties, if I focus on acquiring twenty-four listings or four hundred listings, I will reach my goal. The agent does this backward and starts buying buyer lead thinking that will lead them to their goal.

As a leading real estate coach, I've had the honor of working with the top 200 teams in North America, and I've seen many buyer-heavy transaction teams struggle to show a strong profit. A listing-heavy team will sell 300 properties and have a higher profit margin than a buyer-focused team that sells 900.

Read on to learn about my streamlined approach to focusing on listings.

THE LISTING SALES PROCESS

Before we get started, here is an overview of the listing process. I've included our listing process checklist at the end of this chapter.

- Listing Leads
- Seller Intake Form
- Pre-Appointment Preparation
- Listing Appointment and Close
- Listing Execution (which includes paperwork after listing plans)

LISTING LEAD GENERATION

The first step in the listing sales process is generating leads. This is where you showcase your marketing USPs and Risk Reversals to attract potential home sellers. The goal of this step is to make them aware of your services and why they should choose you as their listing agent. As a team leader, you must focus 80% of your marketing efforts and dollars on listing-lead generation. Teams that spend 80% of their marketing dollars on buyer-lead generation will struggle.

INTAKE PROCESS

At the heart of the listing process is the intake process. This is when your team first encounters a potential home seller. You must have a standardized intake process, including a seller information sheet and a known phone script, to gather information and prepare for a successful appointment.

Train your entire team, from buyer specialists to listing coordinators and receptionists on how to fill out an intake form and the most critical questions to ask. The entire organization needs to be trained to talk to a property owner and capture critical information so the team can acquire a future listing client. It is a mistake to have your people simply take their name, number, and e-mail and pass that along to an agent. The agent will see this opportunity as a lead and not elevate it to the urgency and importance of a ready-to-list person.

We have a simple form we fill out on every potential listing client. This form should be filled out fully no matter how far away the property owner is from selling their home, as all owners will eventually sell. The input sheet should be entered into the Client Relationship Management (CRM) system and assigned to the proper person who will follow up and work toward conversion.

Here are the most important questions on your seller intake sheet:

- Name, Number, E-mail: Can I please get all the owners' names, best numbers, and e-mail?

- Source: Who should we thank for you reaching out to us today? Or, how did you hear about us?
- Mailing address and selling property address. What is your property address? Do you own any other properties?
- How long have you owned the property?
- When you decide to sell, what will your goal be?
- Where will you go when your property is sold?
- How soon would you like to be there?
- Do you know what properties like yours are selling for in your neighborhood?
- End the conversation with, "Great! What I recommend we do is set up an appointment to tour your property. That way we can give you a complete property equity report showing you what your property would sell for in today's market using our marketing strategies. What day works best for you?"

PHONE SCRIPTS

There are two types of phone calls that you and your team need to be trained on. An outbound phone call means you are dialing out to an owner and an inbound phone call is where a potential client calls you.

Mastery: Have scripts, but let your team know they can make small adjustments so the words feel more natural to the speaker. When you force your team to sound like you, the clients feel it. Something will seem off.

> Trust your team to understand the concept and use their own voice to get the message across.

Examples of outbound calling will be when you are circle prospect-calling a neighborhood of owners informing them of a new listing in their neighborhood. You can also do this when there is an upcoming open house, expired listings, canceled listings, for sale by owner, and a new closing.

We also capture the buyer's information when we sell a listing. This is often referred to as adopting a buyer. You did not represent the buyer in the purchase, you represented the seller. However, 90% of all buyers never hear from their agent again after closing.

> **$1M:** If you collect the buyer's information, you and your team can easily follow up six months after closing and establish a relationship with the buyer. Now you have a future listing. We have done this in the past and listed homes within the same year of the buyer's purchase. They literally say they chose us to list it because we were the agents who sold them the house. They remembered our sign in the yard and their buyer's agent forgot to follow up.

Your inbound phone calls come from signs, radio ads, billboards, Google Business Page, and other online sources. These are golden calls and you can't afford to miss them. I often joke with my coaching clients—but it is absolutely true—

if I were to move to their marketplace I wouldn't need leads, I would just need their missed call report.

> **Mastery:** It is critical that you have a separate phone number for your major marketing sources. That way you can track all the seller inbound calls and return any missed calls that happened.

In all cases, reach out to homeowners with compelling offers and reasons for them to want to meet with your team.

Here are compelling reasons a homeowner should want to meet with your team:

- Your team can tell them how much equity they have in their home.
- Your team can advise them on how to improve the value of their home.
- Your team can tell them how long it would take to sell their home.

Here is an example of these offers in action:

> "Hi, 'OWNER,' this is 'AGENT'S NAME,' the reason I'm calling is to offer a no-cost home equity report showing you not only your home's value but how much equity you have in your home. Would that be valuable financial information for you to have?"

The following scripts should be used to gather information from the homeowner and set expectations for the upcoming meeting.

"Hi, 'OWNER,' this is 'AGENT'S NAME,' and the reason I'm calling is to see if you are planning any remodeling projects for your home. If so, would it be helpful for our team to give you an upgrade report showing you the top areas that will improve the value of your home?"

"Hi, 'OWNER', this is 'AGENT'S NAME,' The reason I'm calling is that many homeowners are wondering how the market is doing and how long it will take if they ever decide to list their homes. Would it be helpful for you to know how long it would take to sell your home?"

Gather all information on the property that you can. You will need to complete a market analysis because you will show up prepared with a report. The most important information is bedroom count, bathroom count, year built, square footage, lot size, what improvements they have made since it last sold, and what they believe are the most important features of the property.

PRE-APPOINTMENT PREPARATION

Always be prepared to list your home when going on the home tour, even if the homeowner is far from selling. On our team, we only believe what people do, not what they say, and if they have invited you to their house, they are likely open to the idea of listing. Be sure to have all necessary materials, comparable sales, listing presentations, and all listing documents in a branded professional folder.

I've made millions of dollars just for showing up prepared when the competition shows up with a notepad or, even worse, nothing.

Here are some questions your listing agents should ask before the appointment:

- How long have you owned the property?
- Do you own any other properties?
- What is your goal?
- Where are you going next?
- Will all decision-makers be present?
- Have you received any advice from another agent?

LISTING APPOINTMENT

The listing appointment is broken up into two phases. These phases can happen on the same day or a day apart.

Phase 1 – The Home Tour

The first phase is the property tour. It's important to train your agents on how to conduct this tour, as it's critical to maintain rapport with the owner during this stage. The goal is to build trust and establish a positive relationship with the homeowner.

Do not break rapport during the tour; this is the time to get to know the property and take notes.

Don't give advice during the home tour. Pointing out flaws, even if it is constructive, breaks rapport and gives the agent a false sense of adding value. People believe they have the best home and don't want you to point out the flaws. They want an agent who loves their home.

There is a time and place for constructive criticism and advice, and that is after they commit to listing with your team.

Remember that time kills deals. If the listing presentation doesn't happen at the time of the tour, it should be scheduled as soon as possible. Our standard is to schedule the next appointment within twenty-four hours or, when competing, after the last agent.

Phase 2 – The Listing Presentation

The second phase is the listing presentation. This is where you go over your marketing and value propositions, present a market analysis, and run the numbers with the owner. It's crucial to be prepared with paperwork and have all the necessary materials ready for the presentation.

You have the homeowner's undivided attention until you give them the value and commission. You want to hang onto that information until after you have completed your listing presentation.

There are three outcomes to a listing presentation—they list with you, they list with someone else, or they decide to list at an unknown date in the future.

After years of experience tracking thousands of appointments, I have found that most owners only meet with one agent, so if you are there with the owner, it is yours to screw up.

> **Framework:** If you find yourself competing for a listing, always be the last agent to present the information and ask for the listing. You are more likely to get the contract if you do this.

To avoid screwing up, follow up! After the listing appointment—even if the homeowner doesn't list their home at the time of the presentation—they will likely move forward in the next twenty-four hours. It is important to have a follow-up sequence designed for the 24 hours after the appointment. Every day that passes decreases the owner's likelihood of listing. I've found that one-third of owners list during the appointment or within the next twenty-four hours, one-third list in the next six months, and one-third past six months. So, follow up!

> **$1M:** Follow up!

ONE-STEP VERSUS TWO-STEP LISTING APPOINTMENTS

One-Step Listing Appointment

The one-step listing appointment is when both phases of the listing appointment are conducted during the home tour. If everything looks accurate, all decision-makers are present, and there is no competition from other agents, you can ask if the homeowner would like to sit down and review the numbers. The homeowner will always agree because they want to see your numbers. This allows you to transition from phase one (the home tour) into phase two (the listing presentation).

Two-Step Listing Appointment

The two-step listing appointment involves scheduling a separate appointment for the listing presentation. This can be done if the owner is not ready to make a decision at the time of the home tour, or if any additional factors need to be considered before the presentation can be made. Train your team to be able to determine this during the tour.

During the home tour, if the agent feels the numbers are accurate and they are in a position to list the home, move into phase two.

> **Mastery:** Putting off phase two when you are not competing with other agents opens the door for competition.

In either case, it's important to always be prepared and to have all of the necessary materials and paperwork ready for the appointment. This includes a completed CMA, a marketing and value proposition presentation, and a clear contract outlining all terms and conditions. I can't overstate the importance of showing up prepared to do both phases.

Reasons for a Two-Step Listing Appointment

There are several reasons a two-step listing appointment may be necessary:

- **Failure to allow adequate time and preparation:** If you were not fully prepared for the listing appointment, it may be necessary to schedule a follow-up appointment to ensure that you have all necessary materials and paperwork in place.
- **Competition with another agent:** If you find out that you are competing with another agent, it may be best to schedule a two-step appointment to avoid being compared to the other agent during the home tour. Being the last agent to present can often make a lasting impression on the homeowner.
- **Decision makers not present:** If all decision makers are not present during the home tour, it may be necessary to schedule a separate appointment so all decision-makers can be present for the listing presentation.

Now you understand the listing appointment, it's time to learn how to land the client.

ARTICULATING YOUR VALUE

By articulating your value, you can differentiate yourself from other agents and show the owner why you are the best agent to sell their property. This can include highlighting your unique selling points, risk reversals, guarantees, and marketing strategies. During this part of the presentation, it is important to hold off on the valuation numbers to keep the homeowner's focus. By holding off on these numbers until you have established yourself as the right agent for the job, you can ensure that the homeowner has a clear understanding of your value proposition and marketing strategies. Plus, as I said earlier, when you tell them the numbers, you lose their concentration.

When it's time to break down the numbers and present the owner with their walk-away money, or equity, they will likely have already made a decision on whether they want you to be their agent. This is an important step in the listing process because this is what the owner wants to know. The owner doesn't really care what your commission is or the value of their home. The only number they really care about is their equity position. After presenting that number, focus on that number and whether or not it will get them to their goal.

GOING FOR THE CLOSE

After completing the CMA review and running the numbers, it's important to go for the close and ask the homeowner if they want to move forward with the next steps. This includes getting the listing paperwork out of the way, scheduling photos, and planning for the listing process in the future.

Here are some one-liners you can use to close on the listing:

- Let's go ahead and get the paperwork out of the way.
- Would you like to schedule photos?
- Can you list your home today?

- What do you think, can you make the numbers work?
- Do you have an extra set of keys for me?
- Have we gone over enough today that listing your home would be our next step?
- It sounds like you are ready to schedule professional photography.
- Would it be too soon to ask if we can get the paperwork out of the way?
- I really enjoyed seeing your house. To be honest, I'm not sure if we can sell for the price you want but, I would be honored to use our marketing to see if it is possible.
- What date works best for you to get your home listed on the market?

> **$1M:** Have a rule on your team that you never present numbers without asking for the listing.

NEVER HELP WITHOUT A COMMITMENT

It's important to remember that you should never help someone prepare for a listing without a commitment. Helping owners with staging, vendors, repairs, and preparation gives the agent a false sense of gaining a future listing. Once the homeowner extracts all of your knowledge and value, you become, like all the other agents, essentially a commodity. This can result in you losing the listing to another agent for a lower commission, or you gain the listing but they negotiate your fee.

By going for the close, breaking down the numbers, and securing a commitment from the owner before offering advice, you can increase your chances of winning the listing and ensuring a successful sale.

Once the homeowner is ready to list their home, you must have a clear and concise contract. This should outline all disclosures, commission agreements, and any other necessary details.

It's crucial to understand the importance of designing a standardized listing process and training your company to use it. A well-designed and standardized process can help ensure that all team members are on the same page and working toward the same goals.

LISTING COURSE

To assist with the standardization process, I've created a 100-page manual and a listing course. This manual provides in-depth guidance and step-by-step instructions on how to design and implement a successful listing process, making it a valuable resource for agents and teams looking to improve their sales skills. For more information about this course, go to my website.

NEXT STEPS:
HOW TO WIN THE LISTING

- Make phone calls or answer the phone—
  the initial intake phone call.
- Set the first appointment.
- Fill out the pre-appointment questionnaire.
- Go to the appointment prepared to list.
- Do the grand tour.
- Give your soon-to-be client the value presentation.
- Review the market analysis.
- Run the numbers.
- Get the paperwork out of the way. Remember not
  to give advice until after paperwork is signed.
- Set proper expectations. And then stick to them!
- Provide a to-do list prior to the listing going live.
- Brief the Listing Coordinator.

Always go to a property tour with all of the necessary paperwork. Hold off on the numbers until after you explain to them the value of using you as their agent.

Below is an example of our listing checklist that includes before, during, and after procedures.

PRE-APPOINTMENT LISTING
APPOINTMENT CHECKLIST

- ❑ Listing Script
- ❑ Seller Input Sheet (SIS)
- ❑ Set Appointment
- ❑ Pre-Qualification Questions (Test Motivation)
- ❑ Provide Listing Coordinator LC - SIS
- ❑ Brief LC on Listing Package Requirements
- ❑ Prepared Listing Package – LC Prepared (Listing Agreement, Seller Disclosure Form, Legal, Listing Input Sheet, Briefing Sheet, Law of Agency Pamphlet, Lead-Based Paint, Zillow Reviews, and Platinum Listing Flyer)
- ❑ Pre-listing Package to client (Welcome email or video and Listing Package Documents by mail or email)
- ❑ Appointment in Calendar
- ❑ Reminder Call
- ❑ Complete Comparable Market Analysis (CMA)
- ❑ Review CMA with Team Leader or Team Member

LISTING APPOINTMENT
CHECKLIST

❑ Grand Tour (Determine Decision Maker and
   Build Rapport)

❑ Determine 1 Step or 2 Step

   ❑ If 2 Step –
      Set an Appointment to review numbers at the office

   ❑ If 1 Step –
      Sit at Kitchen Table or equivalent

❑ Review Motivation

❑ Seller Counseling Interview

❑ Listing Presentation (Build Value)

❑ CMA—Comparable Market Analysis

❑ Determine Price

❑ Run the Numbers

❑ Close to List

❑ Complete Paperwork

❑ Set Possible Dates for Photos

❑ Keys

❑ Estimate Listing Date Set

❑ Provide Copies Signed Documents

❑ Promise Script or Instruct on How to Give Referrals

❑ Business Card Door to Door 5 Neighbors

AFTER LISTING APPOINTMENT CHECKLIST

- ❑ Brief Listing Coordinator
- ❑ Send Copies to Client
- ❑ Brief Team at Team Meeting
- ❑ Schedule Broker's Tour
- ❑ Deliver Sign and Lockbox Day of Listing
- ❑ Send Thank You Email with Next Expectations
- ❑ Set Reminder Calls to Seller for Each Week
- ❑ Just Listed Phone Calls or Door to Door – 10 to 100 Neighbors
- ❑ Just Pended Phone Calls or Door to Door
- ❑ Just Sold Phone Calls or Door to Door
- ❑ Set Reminder 30 Day Review
- ❑ Set Reminder 60 Day Review
- ❑ Set Reminder 90 Day Review (Extend Listing)
- ❑ Set Reminder 120 Day Review (Extend Listing)
- ❑ Set Reminder 150 Day Review (Extend Listing)

CHAPTER 13

OPTIMIZING THE BUYER SALES PROCESS

A step-by-step guide to converting leads into sales.

In this chapter, we will focus on the process of taking a potential buyer from a new lead to close.

As a real estate agent, I've come to learn that there are few industries with more unproductive time spent and uncontrollable variables than helping a buyer find a home.

John (not his real name) was only able to look at homes on Sundays due to his work schedule. Unfortunately, this conflicted with my love for watching the Seattle Seahawks, which hadn't been good for a while. But, being a devoted agent with goals to reach, I showed John homes every Sunday for 17 weeks straight, missing every single Seahawks game—including the playoff game where Marshawn Lynch did the famous Beast Quake run against the Saints. Ok, sidebar for a second. This event occurred in the fourth quarter while Seattle was up by four points, Lynch rushed for 67 yards and broke nine tackles to score a touchdown, which secured the Seahawks' eventual 41–36 victory. The crowd was so loud there was a recording picked up on the nearest Richter scale.

Anyway, after the Beast Quake, I couldn't contain my frustration any longer. I gently confronted John, asking him if he was genuinely serious about buying a house or if he was just stringing me along. To my surprise, he was shocked by my question. He and his wife thought we were having fun, and they looked forward to house hunting every Sunday. They felt like they were part of a TV show, and it was pure entertainment for them.

This revelation served as a wake-up call for me. I realized that buyers need to follow a process. As an agent, my job is to get people to the finish line, otherwise, it's all wasted time and bad business.

So, I created a process that I now follow with all my clients. This process not only allows me to manage my time more effectively but also ensures that my clients understand the seriousness of the home-buying experience. I can now balance my love for the Seahawks and my dedication to my clients, making my career in real estate more fulfilling and rewarding than ever before.

THE PROACTIVE APPROACH TO BUYER REPRESENTATION

The real estate industry is full of ups and downs, and to be successful in this field, you need to have a combination of unwavering faith and a clear understanding of the current reality. This is where the Stockdale Paradox comes in. The Stockdale Paradox is a term coined by Jim Collins in his book *Good to Great,* and states that you must maintain faith that you will ultimately succeed while also facing the brutal facts of your current situation.

Lead conversion is a critical part of the sales process in real estate. It requires agents to maintain a constant focus on their clients, no matter what challenges they might face. They need to have unwavering faith that they can and will succeed in converting their leads into clients while at the same time being realistic about the challenges they might face along the way.

In real estate, you might encounter leads that are difficult to convert, leads that are uninterested, or even leads that are actively looking to buy or sell a home with someone else. These challenges can be difficult to face but they are a part of the reality of the industry. By embracing the Stockdale Paradox, you can maintain your focus on the end goal and stay committed to following up with your leads until they are converted into clients.

One of the keys to successfully applying the Stockdale Paradox to lead conversion is to have a well-defined follow-up plan. This plan should include a clear strategy for reaching out to your leads, staying in contact with them, and providing them with value-added content that will keep them engaged and interested in working with you.

By having a lead standard, you can stay focused on your goals and avoid getting discouraged by setbacks.

ESTABLISHING LEAD STANDARDS IN THE BUYER SALES PROCESS

As a real estate team, it's important to have a strong and organized lead process in place to help you manage and convert buyer-leads into successful sales. The first step in establishing a lead process is to establish lead standards.

Simply put, a lead standard is the highest level of performance you expect from your team when it comes to generating and managing buyer leads. By setting clear standards, you can help your team focus their efforts and achieve consistent results.

Remember, the largest percentage of your revenue is going to come from listings, but this doesn't mean you should ignore buyers. It just means you need to have a streamlined process to maximize cost-per-lead.

As I have worked with the top teams in North America, the teams with the highest-held standards are always the most profitable. Some teams may have an advantage over the market with a lead source, but if they don't have lead standards and a distribution process, they will lose the leads to other teams fishing in the same pond. If the lead source doesn't produce lower funnel leads, their team won't convert because they don't have a long-term approach to lead conversion.

> **Framework:** The higher the lead is in the sales funnel the better your process and training needs to be, but, here is the secret to profits, the better you are at converting top funnel leads, the more money you will make with less competition.

When establishing lead standards, it's important to start with a realistic and attainable goal. As your team exceeds this goal, you can gradually raise the bar and establish a new standard. This will not only motivate your team to perform at a higher level, but it will also ensure that your lead process remains effective and efficient over time.

Key elements to consider when establishing lead standards for your real estate team:

- **Lead Generation:** Establish clear standards for the number of attempts per new lead and how to categorize each lead based on the result and conversation and what the follow-up process looks like for each category. This will help your team focus their efforts and ensure that they are consistently reaching out to potential buyers. If an agent doesn't meet the set standards, you should nudge them to follow the process. If the agent still doesn't follow the process, you will need to reassign the leads to another agent.

- **Lead Qualification:** Develop a process for qualifying leads to ensure that your team spends their time on the most promising leads. This may include verifying contact information, conducting a preliminary needs assessment, and verifying their level of interest in purchasing a property. The core philosophy for you and your agents should be to help people become qualified versus disqualified. It is important to emphasize that when you start qualifying people too early, before you establish trust, you may break rapport. The most common mistake made by agents is asking qualification questions too early. Asking about the buyer's financing and whether or not they have met with an agent comes across as arrogant and signals that you are too good for the buyer. The buyer will feel like you only care about a sale, not about them. Once trust is established—or when the buyer gives you permission—you must certainly ask about their financing situation and whether or not they have worked with another agent. The best way to ask about financing is to ask if they need help with their financing options. Worried they are working with another agent? Ask the buyer if they have seen any homes they like. If not, the probability that they have an agent is low. Your agents need to seek to understand the person first before their criteria. If you violate this concept the person will feel like you are superior and judging them.

- **Lead Management:** Set clear expectations for how leads should be tracked, managed, and followed up with. This will help to ensure that zero leads fall through the cracks and that your team is able to nurture and convert leads into sales effectively.

Your real estate team needs to achieve consistent and effective results in their buyer sales process. With a clear and organized approach, you can build a strong lead pipeline and close more deals.

Now that we've established the importance of lead standards, it's time to set some specific, measurable goals for your real estate team. As mentioned earlier, it's important to start with a realistic and attainable goal that you can gradually raise over time.

For your team, the baseline lead standards could include:

- Calling all leads within fifteen minutes. This goal helps ensure that your team is quickly and effectively engaging with potential buyers. By calling leads promptly, you can increase your chances of converting them into clients.
- Answering the majority of inbound calls. This goal helps ensure that your team is available and responsive when potential buyers reach out to them. By answering—not

letting voicemail answer for you—a high percentage of calls, you can build trust and credibility with your clients.

- Returning all missed calls. When potential buyers call and don't reach your team, it's important to return their call as soon as possible. This goal helps ensure that your team is following up promptly and effectively with all leads.

- Responding to all messages. Whether it's through email, text, or social media, it's important to respond to all messages from potential buyers in a timely manner. This goal helps ensure that your team is providing excellent customer service and building strong relationships with clients.

By meeting these baseline lead standards, your real estate team will be well on their way to generating and converting more leads into sales. Remember to adjust these to your specific team.

THE POWER OF PROPER LEAD LABELING IN REAL ESTATE

As a real estate professional, it's important to be strategic and intentional in how you approach and label your leads. Labeling a lead as a buyer lead may seem like a harmless designation, but it can actually limit your team's ability to convert that lead into a client.

Why? Because when you label a lead as a buyer lead, your team will naturally start to focus their efforts on selling them a property. But what if that lead doesn't actually want to buy right now? What if they're more interested in selling? If you focus on selling them something, they will be put off and look elsewhere for help.

That's why it's important to find out which leads own property. This information can be obtained through a variety of methods, such as public records searches, online research, or direct communication with the lead. By extracting property owners from your lead database, you can give them a large portion of your attention, value, and follow-up. This can help you build stronger relationships and convert more of these leads into clients.

THE SECRET TO LEAD CONVERSION: TREAT ALL LEADS AS PROPERTY OWNERS

As a real estate agent, your goal is to convert leads into clients. But to do that, you need to understand what motivates these potential clients and what they really want. Contrary to popular belief, nobody wakes up one day and says they want to be a buyer of a property. They wake up and say they want to be a homeowner. This is the key to lead conversion in real estate.

Treat all leads as owners, regardless of their current status as a renter or owner. This means tailoring your scripts, follow-up, content creation, and value-adds around ownership. By doing this, you'll be able to connect with your leads on a deeper level and address their specific needs and goals.

> **Framework:** When you start treating all leads as potential property owners and future sellers, you'll win them over as buyers and be there when they list their property.

It's easy for agents to label themselves as a buyer's agent because that's the only experience their clients have had with them. But the law of primacy kicks in, and clients will see your agency and team as a buyer's team and not a listing team. To establish authority as a listing machine with incredible buyer services, it's important to showcase your team's strengths and expertise in both buying and selling properties.

THE ART OF LEAD MANAGEMENT:
ASSIGNING OPPORTUNITIES
TO YOUR TEAM MEMBERS

In the world of real estate, leads are the lifeblood o5 team that can deliver results for your clients.

A WELL-DEFINED BUYER-SALES PROCESS

When it comes to the buyer sales process, the first agent to set an appointment with the lead gets exclusive rights to the lead.

To start, agents make seven calls to the lead in seven days, using the CRM to track their progress. The goal is to make contact and establish a connection with the lead. If contact is made, there are two possible outcomes: either an appointment is made or it isn't. If an appointment is made, the lead is reported and given priority service. If no appointment is made, the lead is put into a follow-up process, where they must be contacted once a month or risk being reassigned.

If the lead is a property owner, they are reported to the listing department for appropriate handling.

Once an appointment is made, the agent must be a trained specialist, ready to go house hunting and find the perfect home for their new client. Using reverse prospecting and deal-making, the agent must be proactive in their approach to buyer service. A passive approach will result in losing the client to another agent who's more proactive.

Real estate is a competitive market and only the fittest agents survive and get the deal. By following this well-defined process, real estate teams can ensure they're making the most of every opportunity that comes their way.

MONITOR AND RECORD
ALL THINGS POSSIBLE

It is important that you monitor and review the actions of your agents regularly. If you are a solo agent, come up with a process to monitor your own actions. A spot check is all you need to keep your team members on their toes and let them know that you are watching their performance and show that you care about their success.

One important aspect of real estate is phone calls. Recording all your phone calls is crucial in keeping track of your conversations and ensuring that you do not miss out on any potential leads. Have a phone system that has the ability to record phone calls for training and tracking opportunities.

> **Framework:** Know your regulations and laws as it pertains to recording calls and follow the laws.

You and your agents will perform better on the phone knowing the call is being recorded and it gives you the chance to save the best (and worst) calls for training purposes. Share recorded calls during weekly sales training so other agents can learn from each other. Focus on the process of the call, not the result. To do this, review the calls and don't disclose the outcome. Giving the outcome distorts the skill and agent's discipline to follow the process. Think of it like this, if you share a bad call where the agent does everything wrong but gets lucky with a hot buyer, you teach the wrong thing. That example doesn't teach anyone about how to improve their client calls. Find the call where the agent does everything right but the buyer just isn't ready yet and the agent shares how they plan to follow up and take long-term action to win the client over. When new agents come on board, you can have them listen to dozens of great and not-so-great calls. You and your agents will not typically lose opportunities for something you did say, you lose because of something you didn't say.

A daily call report and an inbound phone call report can help you keep track of all the calls received and missed by your team.

Every missed call is a lead and it's your responsibility as a team leader to make sure that they are called back as soon as possible. In the real estate business, missed calls can be a goldmine for leads. The reason for this is simple—people only call when they are looking for something. Whether it's for information about a property or an appointment, it is a missed opportunity if you don't return the call.

I can attest that calling back missed calls has returned millions in revenue.

NEXT STEPS: HOW TO OPTIMIZE YOUR BUYER SALES PROCESS

- Make a realistic and attainable goal that your team can agree on.
- Consider your leads as opportunities.
- Have a solid process for who returns missed calls.
- Consider using a service that can record your phone calls and use logs to keep information tracked.
- Treat all leads as potential buyers.

In the end, remember that real estate teams make most of their profit from listings, but the buyer-lead conversion process—with proper follow-up—will be a listing in the future. That is why we spend so much time, money, and effort on buyer-lead conversion. Never lose sight of the ultimate goal, a lifetime client relationship.

CHAPTER 14

BUILDING A STRONG FOUNDATION

The importance of a robust operations core for real estate team leaders.

In this chapter, we will focus on maximizing efficiency and ensuring compliance through a dedicated support staff.

The first time I truly understood the importance of team-work was during my early days as a solo real estate agent. I remember the exact moment when everything changed. I had been working alone, handling every aspect of my real estate business. I was confident in my abilities and certain that I could handle anything that came my way. That was until I signed my first-ever million-dollar listing in Hawk's Meadows.

Hawk's Meadows is a luxurious, picturesque neighborhood overlooking Lake Chelan. Back then, I was taking the bus to save gas money, and the only car I could borrow for the listing appointment was my mother-in-law's Honda CRV. Though it was a massive upgrade from my green Subaru, I still parked it around the corner from the mansion, too embarrassed to let the seller see it.

I had given it my all to win the listing. I promised the seller a custom website, that a listing agent would accompany all showings with the buyer's agents, broker's tours, open houses each weekend, a custom-built sign, video tours, staging, pre-inspection, and bi-weekly updates. After securing the listing, I spent the next thirty days juggling all these tasks, trying to fulfill each promise I had made to the seller.

Despite my best efforts, after the 180-day listing contract, the house didn't sell. I had not only spent thousands of dollars on marketing and services, but I had also lost countless hours that could have been spent prospecting and acquiring more clients. My business suffered because I was too focused on servicing one single listing instead of working on growing my company.

I knew then that I needed a team to help me conquer the real estate world. I needed a core group of people who could divide and conquer, ensuring that each task was handled efficiently and professionally. I realized that, with the right team, I could have still acquired that million-dollar listing and handed off the operational details to my staff, allowing me to focus on acquiring more clients.

Even if the house still hadn't sold, having a team behind me would have ensured the growth of my company. Today, I am grateful to the people who have helped me become a visionary leader, working on the business instead of being consumed by it.

THE CORE

Real estate teams need support staff to keep the sales agents on track and ensure compliance with industry regulations. The support staff is known as The Core, and they play a vital role in the team's success.

The Core key positions: listing coordination, closing coordination, Director of Sales, Director of Inside Sales, Director of Marketing, Director of Human Resources, and a managing broker for compliance.

The broker serves as the director for both listing and closing coordination as they must have access to all files in the system for compliance purposes and to provide feedback to sales management.

The listing coordination department is responsible for all the logistical execution of the listing process and support of the listing agents. The listing coordination process should enhance the client experience and increase the capacity of the agents to go out and produce more listings for the company.

The closing coordination department is responsible for the closure of all contracts and communication with third parties. They will enhance the client relationship and experience and provide support and leverage for agents so that they can focus on client acquisition.

Teams and brokerages can lose sight of the main purpose of these positions and fall victim to thinking they are a service and experience enhancers of the agents. This can have unintended consequences where the agent is regularly passing the buck to the support staff without maintaining their responsibilities as the fiduciary. The symbiotic relationship between agent and support staff is healthiest when the support staff relies on the agents to acquire more business to maintain job security and upward mobility of their career, and the agent relies on the support staff to integrate and execute the non-dollar producing activities.

Maintaining great compliance and providing feedback to sales management is crucial for improving training and correcting errors. This is because quality leads to quantity in the real estate industry, and reducing errors before they reach the core can save the team money and increase productivity.

The Core is seen as a way to leverage the sales agent and reduce their workload. However, sales agents must also improve their performance in order to reduce the workload of The Core. If not, the team's payroll will increase, leading to financial loss due to the support staff having to address preventable errors.

EXECUTIVE ASSISTANTS AND TEAM LEADERS

The top producer, who is likely the founder and TL of a real estate team, plays a critical role in the success of the team. As long as the team leader is in production, they must have an executive assistant to help manage their workload and duties.

As the team grows, the TL must systematically remove themselves from production. To relieve these duties, the TL needs to replace themselves with a listing partner. Ideally, this person has trained under the TL for at least two years.

ADDITIONAL KEY POSITIONS

As a real estate team grows, there are several key positions that should be added to The Core to further improve efficiencies and control. One such position is an in-house photographer and videographer. These people are responsible for taking high-quality photos and videos of listings. This will help to reduce the cost-per-listing and improve the overall quality of the team's offerings.

Another important addition to The Core is a Director of Sales. This person is in charge of agent accountability, lead management, and training. They help ensure that the sales agents are meeting their goals and providing the highest level of customer service.

The team should also consider adding a Director of Recruiting, who is responsible for attracting, contacting, and hiring new agents to the team.

The Director of ISA is also important, as they help to manage the day-to-day operations of the ISA team.

Finally, as the team grows to over $5 million annually, it may be beneficial to bring marketing in-house with a Director of Marketing. This person is responsible for creating and executing marketing strategies to help the team reach its goals and continue to grow.

DAY-TO-DAY FOUNDATIONS

A daily huddle is a key aspect of any successful real estate team's operations. This brief meeting can take place in person or online, is an opportunity for the entire core to come together and share important information, priorities, and updates. This meeting is for the support staff but a similar meeting can be used for your outside sales agents to align everyone. I do not recommend combining both support staff and agents in the daily huddle. These should be run separately to avoid drawn-out conversations and wasting everyone's time on information that doesn't pertain to them.

Framework: The daily huddle should be no longer than 15 minutes, allowing the team to stay focused and avoid getting bogged down in lengthy discussions. During the meeting, each person in The Core announces their primary focus for the day or week, ensuring that everyone is working toward the same goals and objectives. This helps to reduce misunderstandings, improve communication, and increase overall productivity.

In addition to discussing priorities, the daily huddle also provides an opportunity for team members to communicate key information. This can include updates on current projects, any potential roadblocks or issues, and any other important news that needs to be shared. The daily huddle is also an opportunity for the team to discuss any impediments or issues that need to be addressed. This can be done in a quick and efficient manner, helping to resolve any problems quickly and prevent them from becoming larger issues down the road.

END-OF-DAY REPORTS

End-of-day reports are an essential part of a successful real estate team's operations. These reports provide a clear and concise summary of the day's activities, helping to keep everyone on the same page and informed about what's going on in the business.

The end-of-day reports should be completed by the real estate team's operation core and submitted to the director.

This helps to ensure that the director, or manager, has a clear understanding of what has been accomplished, what needs to be done, and what, if any, potential roadblocks or issues are causing slowdowns.

In addition to being submitted to the director or manager, end-of-day reports can also be shared with other team members or parties who can benefit from the information. This is known as dual reporting and helps to increase transparency and improve communication within the team.

Here is an example of an end-of-day report from a closing coordinator.

- **New Contracts:** Seller's Name, Buyer's Name, Agent's Name, Address, Price, Closing Date, Notes
- **Closings:** Seller's Name, Buyer's Name, Agent's Name, Address, Price, Commission, Notes
- **Fall Throughs:** Seller's Name, Buyer's Name, Agent's Name, Address, Price, Reason
- **Extension:** Seller's Name, Buyer's Name, Agent's Name, Address, Price, Closing Date, Notes
- **Notes:** What is holding us back? Issues, Concerns?

The same concept can also be used for:

- Listing coordinators to report new listings, commissions, key performance indicators, and issues
- Inside sales calls, reporting contacts, and appointments
- The Director of Sales, reporting calls, contacts, recruits, and meetings

The key to end-of-day reports is to keep them simple, easy to fill out, and acknowledge receipt and provide feedback. The surefire way to annoy and lose trust is to ask for something and not give feedback. Your staff will start to assume you are not reading the reports and that will turn into a lack of trust because they will start to think you don't care. If you don't care, why should they?

As General Maddox discusses in his book, *Call Sign Chaos,* it's important to consider three key questions when communicating information: What do you know? Who needs to know it? And, do they know it? By ensuring that all relevant parties are aware of what is happening in the business, the team can stay aligned and focused on their goals and objectives.

NEXT STEPS:
HOW TO BUILD A STRONG FOUNDATION

- Establish The Core by assembling a team of support staff, including a listing coordinator, closing coordinator, and managing broker for compliance. Ensure that the broker has access to all files in the system for compliance purposes and to provide feedback to sales management.
- As the team grows, add key positions such as an in-house photographer and video staff, Director of Sales, Director of Recruiting, Director of ISA, and a Director of Marketing (if the team grows to over $5 million).
- Hold daily huddles to keep the team focused, aligned, and informed. The huddle should be no longer than

15 minutes and provide an opportunity for team members to communicate key information, priorities, and updates.

- Encourage the operation core to complete end-of-day reports and submit them to the director or direct report. Dual reporting can be implemented to increase transparency and improve communication within the team.
- Follow General Maddox's principles of knowing what you know, who needs to know it, and making sure they know it. This will help to ensure that everyone is aware of what is happening in the business and working toward the same goals and objectives.

The Core is a vital part of a real estate team and helps to keep the sales agents on track, maintain compliance, and provide feedback for improvement. A well-functioning Core can have a significant impact on the success of a real estate team.

Today, as I reflect on that journey, I can't help but be thankful for the lesson I learned from that first million-dollar listing. It taught me the importance of collaboration, delegation, and the power of teamwork. With a solid team, I am confident that you can elevate and grow your business, making a mark in the world of real estate.

CHAPTER 15

HIGH PERFORMERS

Building a real estate team from initial onboarding to continuous training and accountability.

In this chapter, we will discuss mastering the art of sales and professional development through systematic training and peer support.

As a commercial pilot, all of your fellow pilots have passed the necessary standards and obtained their licenses. The question then becomes how do you outperform others when you compete with the same level of talent?

The onboarding system and training departments are instrumental in setting a company apart from others. While working for Focus Air Cargo, I discovered the importance of ensuring no standard was overlooked and the value of training everyone to each standard while only signing off on those who demonstrated proficiency.

Dave McLane, the Director of Training and my mentor, had not only flown Boeing 747s in the Air Force but was also assigned to Air Force One, flying President Clinton and President Bush for eight years. With his vast experience and knowledge, Dave stressed the importance of hiring for aptitude, the willingness and ability to learn, as well as demonstrating appetite—a passion for the job and the desire to work, even for free.

I learned that it wasn't enough to teach something once and expect perfect performance. Instead, the key to success in aviation lay in ensuring that every team member was trained and assessed against the highest standards, time and time again. This was the secret sauce that separated the great airlines from the good ones, and it became a guiding principle in my career.

Dave would make sure that each new pilot was carefully assessed for aptitude and appetite, and emphasized the importance of maintaining strict training standards. Dave knew that when pilots left the training department, he might not see them again for six months. During that time, their skills and adherence to procedures would diverge from the standards. He also knew that if the company allowed subpar standards in the field, they would get below-standard performance. These below-the-line performances would cost the company money and put people's lives at risk, personally and financially.

Dave taught me that each pilot impacts everyone at the company. Likewise, in real estate, each team member impacts everyone at the company. The exceptionally trained group of pilots allowed the start-up airline to be born and take flight. The airline eventually failed due to economic impacts, high oil prices, and outdated and inefficient equipment.

In *The Talent Code,* author Daniel Coyle explores the secrets of the world's best athletes and musicians and the unique ways they develop their skills to reach mastery. The book sheds light on the value of deep practice and the techniques that can be used to cultivate talent in any field.

As a team leader in real estate, I have always been fascinated by this concept and how it can be applied to sales training. My goal is to create a team of top-performing agents who are knowledgeable, confident, and independent in their abilities.

One of the key lessons I learned from *The Talent Code* is the importance of creating an environment that encourages deep practice. This means providing opportunities for my team to engage in challenging, deliberate, and meaningful activities that will help them develop their sales skills and real estate knowledge.

One of the ways I do this is by emboldening my team. I want them to be able to work on their own, without my constant supervision. I provide them with resources, training materials, and opportunities to work on their own—making mistakes and learning from them in the process. This not only helps them develop their skills, but it also builds their confidence and independence.

Another way I apply the principles of *The Talent Code* is by encouraging my team to embrace feedback and use it to grow. I provide regular coaching and mentoring sessions to help my team members identify areas for improvement and develop strategies for reaching their goals.

Finally, I also celebrate their successes and reward their hard work. This reinforces their efforts and encourages them to keep pushing themselves to reach higher levels of mastery.

This has led to the creation of a team of top-performing real estate agents who are confident, independent, and skilled. It's a journey that requires patience, dedication, and a commitment to excellence. It also requires you to step back and let people work. That can be difficult at times, but trust your team. The results will speak for themselves.

PREDICTABLE TRAINING

As a successful real estate team leader, I know that the foundation of success is a strong training program. Since 2012, I have dedicated myself to providing my team with the tools, knowledge, and support they need to succeed in the real estate industry.

We hold training meetings a minimum of four days a week and people often ask what we talk about at our training sessions, but this misses the point. The pressure isn't on me to come up with topics to discuss; instead, it's my job to tap into the voices of my team and bring out the challenges and issues that need training. I use a Socratic method to engage my team in discussion and encourage them to share their experiences, thoughts, and questions.

At the end of the day, real estate training is not just about imparting knowledge and skills, it's about creating a culture of learning, growth, and excellence. By dedicating ourselves to training, my team and I have built a foundation for success that has withstood the test of time.

If you approach your training with the same level of importance as the most critical event of your day, and always seek out new insights and strategies, you too can build a foundation for success that will last for years to come.

ELITE ONBOARDING

As a successful real estate team leader, I understand that having an elite onboarding program is critical to the success of every new agent who joins our team. Whether they are newly licensed or experienced, every agent deserves the support, guidance, and training they need to reach their full potential.

That's why I have the new hire's first thirty days at the company lined out. We focus on getting our new agents into production, meeting our standards, and exceeding their own expectations. Our onboarding program is designed to provide a smooth transition into our team and our culture and to help agents hit the ground running.

The key to a successful onboarding program is to focus on the process, not just the results. While it's important to set high expectations, I don't expect any results for the first 90 days. Instead, I expect my new agents to work hard and get better every day at following and executing our processes.

One of the major components of our onboarding program is the indoctrination of the new agent into our culture. I want to make sure that each new agent feels welcomed, safe, and ready to take action. That's why I take the time to create connections and build relationships with them. I want them to know that they are part of our team and that we are all working together to achieve success.

The goal of our onboarding program is to provide new agents with the tools, knowledge, and support they need to succeed.

This includes training on the latest real estate strategies and techniques, as well as one-on-one coaching and mentorship to help them develop their skills and reach their full potential.

Creating and implementing an elite onboarding program is essential to the success of any real estate team. By providing new agents with the guidance, training, and support they need to succeed, you can help them hit the ground running and achieve their full potential. With a focus on the process and the indoctrination of the new agent into the culture, you can create a team of successful agents who are driven, confident, and ready to take on any challenge.

NO ONE STOPS LEARNING & GROWING

As a real estate team leader, I firmly believe no agent ever graduates from training. The same way pilots in the aviation industry must continually train and show proficiency to stay sharp, real estate agents must also continue to refine their skills and stay on top of industry changes.

At our team, we have a recurrent training schedule to make sure our agents are correcting any bad habits and shortcuts that they may have developed in the field. One of the key benefits of this training is that it helps agents, both new and experienced, avoid making mistakes. New agents tend to make mistakes due to a lack of experience, while experienced agents may make mistakes due to complacency or taking shortcuts. Now all of my team members can stay on top of their game and avoid costly mistakes.

When developing your training plan, think about training in three areas, knowledge, skill, and process. The departments receiving each training will be contracts, the listing process, and buying process. As you dive into training, you will touch on sales skills, influence, negotiation, business fundamentals, real estate core knowledge, and company policies.

While our meetings and training are not mandatory, they are highly encouraged and seen as an important part of our team culture. Our agents understand that ongoing training and development is essential to their success and the success of our team as a whole. However, they also have work to do and are excused without fear of retaliation if they miss a few.

KNOWLEDGE IN BUCKETS

As a real estate team leader, I believe that effective training is key to the success of our team. That's why we have structured our training into four distinct buckets, each with a specific focus to help our agents achieve their full potential. I have found that meetings under 40 minutes achieve the highest retention rates and results in agents taking action afterward. When a subject requires more than forty minutes to train, plan a multi-day event or a block of time with adequate breaks. Any time you have multiple sessions, the key is to build momentum, ending on a high note. When you allow meetings and training to go longer than required, you lose momentum and leadership equity from your people. Top performers don't like wasting time and you must instill in your people a sense of urgency.

- Monday, we focus on real estate contracts, agreements, and knowledge. This is the foundation of our business, and it's critical that all of our agents are up-to-date with the latest information and knowledge in this area.
- Tuesday is dedicated to motivation, mindset, and team information. This is an important day for our agents as it helps them to stay focused on their goals, maintain a positive attitude, and stay connected with the rest of the team.
- Wednesday is sales training day. We focus on the art of selling and our agents have the opportunity to learn from experienced sales professionals and hone their own skills.
- Thursday is procedural training day where we focus on the tools, systems, and process proficiency. This day is critical for making sure our agents have the skills and knowledge they need to operate efficiently and effectively, and provide the best possible service to our clients.
- We don't do training on Fridays.

At the end of each training, we allow time for feedback and discussion. This is a great opportunity for our agents to share their challenges, issues, and successes with the rest of the team. This information is then used to guide the next meeting, ensuring that our training remains relevant and up-to-date.

Our structured training approach is an essential part of our team's success. By dedicating specific days to specific areas of focus, we can ensure that our agents have the knowledge, skills, and motivation they need to perform at their best.

ACCOUNTABILITY

As the team grows, it becomes more difficult for the team leader to hold every individual accountable, which is why accountability groups are essential. These groups are composed of two to six team members that are paired up and hold each other accountable for meeting their goals and following through on their commitments.

Within our culture of accountability, we hold accountability sprints. These are a two to six-week program that replaces Thursday's training and focuses on individual team members committing to action items and being held accountable by their peers. The goal is to create a supportive and motivational environment where everyone is working toward their individual goals while also being held accountable by the team.

At the end of each week, team members must report their results to the other members of their team. This is a critical component of the accountability sprint as it allows for feedback and helps to identify any roadblocks that may be preventing individuals from meeting their goals. Instead of focusing solely on results, the emphasis is on the process, and the results are used to gain insight into what is getting in the way of success.

Incorporating accountability groups into your training program can create an environment where everyone feels responsible for their own success and the success of their team, while simultaneously gaining support to improve their weaknesses and supporting others in theirs.

Ultimately, a strong culture of accountability can create a high-performing real estate team where everyone is working together toward a common goal, while also being held accountable for their individual performance.

NEXT STEPS: HOW TO BUILD A HIGH-PERFORMANCE TEAM

- Create a weekly team meeting agenda framework that covers;
  - Goals
  - Sales
  - New Listings
  - Announcements
  - Acknowledgments
  - Action Items
- Develop a Listing Department training program for the year, including topics like;
  - Listing Strategies
  - Pricing Strategies
  - Marketing Techniques
  - Staging and Photography
  - Negotiation Skills
  - Client Communication and Follow-up
  - The Listing Process
  - The Listing Presentation
  - Farming and Promotion for Listing Strategies

- Develop a Buyer Department training program for the year, including topics such as;

  - Understanding Buyers' Needs and Preferences
  - Effective Home Search Techniques
  - Writing Competitive Offers
  - Negotiating with Sellers
  - Assisting Clients with Inspections and Appraisals
  - Closing the Transaction

- Develop a Contract and Agreement training program for the year, covering topics such as;

  - Purchase Agreements
  - Listing Agreements
  - Disclosure Requirements
  - Addendums and Contingencies
  - Legal Compliance and Risk Management
  - Contract Negotiation Strategies

- Develop a Motivation Mindset training program, focusing on;

  - Goal Setting and Achieving

> **$1M:** Most people are great at setting goals! The people who actually complete their goals are the ones who make it to the top. Teach your team to complete the goals they set.

  - Time Management Techniques
  - Overcoming Challenges and Setbacks
  - Building a Positive Team Culture

- ◆ Continuous Self-improvement and Education
- ◆ Effective Communication and Collaboration

- Prepare a comprehensive onboarding checklist for new agents, including;

  - ◆ Enrollment and Licensing Requirements
  - ◆ Access to the Multiple Listing Service (MLS)
  - ◆ Company Email, Software, and Tools Setup
  - ◆ Training on Company Procedures and Policies
  - ◆ Introduction to Team Members and Mentors
  - ◆ Establishing a Sphere of Influence and Prospecting Plan

- List all knowledge and skills required for top-performing agents, such as;

  - ◆ Market Expertise
  - ◆ Strong Negotiation Skills
  - ◆ Excellent Customer Service
  - ◆ Proficiency in CRM and Marketing Tools
  - ◆ Effective Prospecting Techniques
  - ◆ Time Management and Organization Skills

- Schedule start dates for new classes throughout the year, ensuring consistent training opportunities for both new and existing team members.

- Market and recruit for these class start dates, using various strategies like;

  - ◆ Social Media Campaigns
  - ◆ Email Marketing
  - ◆ Networking Events

- Referral Incentives
- Partnering with Real Estate Schools
- Print and Online Advertising

By following these steps, you can build a high-performing real estate team that is knowledgeable, confident, and independent. A strong year-long training program, elite onboarding, recurrent training, knowledge in buckets, and a culture of accountability will help you and your team achieve success and reach mastery in the real estate industry.

CHAPTER 16

CREATING RAVING FANS

The importance of customer service, experience obsession, and social proof.

In this chapter, we will discuss how to build a strong reputation and grow your business through exceptional customer care.

There I was, on a layover in the bustling city of Bangkok, utterly unaware of what was about to unfold. On my first day there, I ventured out to explore the temples and landmarks throughout the city. Little did I know, I would become a target for an elaborate con.

As I walked down a busy street, I was approached by a friendly-looking man who introduced himself as Ake. We struck up a conversation and he eventually mentioned a unique event happening that day. According to Ake, it was a special day sanctioned by the president, during which blue sapphires from a recently closed mine could be sold at an unbeatable price. Ake gave me a tourist map showing me all the best temples to visit while in Bangkok and called a tuk-tuk to give me a ride on my journey. I thought it was exciting and incredible how nice and helpful people in Bangkok were, and I continued on my way, giving it little thought.

Later in the day, I found myself at a temple where I met Suda, a charming woman. She casually mentioned the same blue sapphire event that Ake had mentioned earlier. My curiosity was piqued, but I still didn't pay it too much mind.

As I meandered through the city, I eventually encountered a third person who mentioned the sapphire sale. This time, it was a friendly tuk-tuk driver who happened to mention the event while we chatted during my ride. With three separate people raving about this rare opportunity, I couldn't resist the pull of social proof any longer. I had to get one of these elusive blue sapphires for myself.

Following the driver's directions, I ended up at a small jewelry shop tucked away in a side alley. The charismatic owner showed me a stunning blue sapphire and, after a bit of negotiation, I purchased it for $2,000. I left the store feeling accomplished and proud to have acquired such a beautiful gemstone.

Back home, reality set in as I discovered that the sapphire I had purchased was worth nowhere near what I paid for it—likely worth less than a piece of jewelry you could buy at Target. I had been expertly conned. It was a hard lesson to learn, but it made me realize the power of social proof and the significance of having raving fans.

In the world of real estate, we can apply this concept ethically to our advantage. It's not about knowing people, but rather, knowing people who will genuinely sing your praises to others. Positive testimonials, five-star reviews, and word-of-mouth recommendations can act as a form of social proof, making potential clients more likely to choose your company.

Just as the intricate con in Bangkok relied on multiple sources confirming the same information to make it seem true, a strong network of happy clients can help to establish your company as a trusted and reliable choice in the competitive real estate market. The difference is, the bill of goods you are selling is actually worth the price.

In today's world, customers are more empowered than ever before. They are more informed, more connected, and more demanding. They want to feel valued, heard, and appreciated.

It's up to real estate teams to anticipate and understand these needs and deliver an exceptional experience every step of the way.

This is why customer service is the backbone of a successful real estate business. From the initial phone call to the final walk-through, each interaction with a client has the potential to make or break the experience. Because real estate transactions can be a complex and emotional journey for buyers and sellers, team leaders must ensure that every touchpoint is seamless, personal, and memorable.

As the years pass, your clients may not remember how much money they made or how you saved the deal, but they will remember how they felt. With so much at stake, it's essential that the client experience is given the highest priority.

THE CLIENT'S JOURNEY

The client's journey is the series of interactions a client has with a real estate team from the moment they first make contact to the successful completion of the transaction.

In the book, *Outside In*, authors Harley Manning and Kerry Bodine stress the importance of putting customers first. They highlight the need for companies to think about their customer's journey and to understand their pain points. They argue that if companies can solve these customer pain points, they will be able to create a better experience for their customers and ultimately increase their satisfaction and loyalty.

For real estate teams, the client's journey starts with the initial consultation. This is where the team gets to know the buying client, their needs, and what they are looking for in their next property (for a selling client, why they want to sell their property). It's important to establish a rapport with the client and to make them feel comfortable. The team should listen actively, ask questions, and be responsive to their needs.

Once the client has made their decision to move forward, the team will take them through the home search or listing process. This can be a stressful time for clients and it's important that the team is on hand to answer any questions they may have.

> **Framework:** For a buyer, make sure you have plenty of properties to show them. For a seller, make sure you know what the current market is doing. The goal is to make your client feel at ease.

The next stage of the client's journey is the negotiation process. This is where the team works hard to get the best deal for their client. The team should be transparent, honest, and professional in dealing with the other agent. They should also keep their client updated at every stage of the negotiation and closing process. There is no greater way to be fired from a client than to fail to communicate with them in a timely manner. Surveys have shown that clients want an update from their agent on a daily basis. That is unrealistic for a top producer but it is possible once the agent understands that the clients don't need new information, they just need to be contacted. Most client check-ins are to get a feel for their emotional state.

Here are the key stages your client will need updates on, the initial offer, counter offers, in between communication with the other agent, accepted or rejected offers, opening or closing escrow, home inspection, appraisal updates, missing information, title report review, final items, schedule signing, closing day, receiving keys, and celebration. The most important part of the buying/selling process is the final forty-eight hours, which are riddled with unexpected items and emotions are high. The team needs to be the rock in a turbulent sea. The team and agent need to get the clients to the finish line and—once it is all over—they will forget about the turbulence and be happy they made it safely.

Once the transaction is completed, the team moves on to the post-sale stage. This is where the team should take the time to check in with the client and see how they are settling into their new home. The team should also be there to answer any questions they may have and to offer their support.

> **Framework:** A single person can handle most of these interactions, but it should be clear to the client that while they may see only a handful of people from your real estate group, there is a whole team behind them, supporting them.

The client's journey is a critical aspect of the real estate sales process. Real estate teams need to be obsessed with checking in on the client experience in every critical phase. By doing so, they will be able to deliver an exceptional experience that will keep their clients coming back.

NET PROMOTER SCORES

Net Promoter Score (NPS) is a powerful tool real estate teams can use to measure the satisfaction of their clients throughout the client's journey and improve their overall experience.

An NPS is a customer satisfaction metric that measures the likelihood a client will recommend a company or product to others. It's calculated by asking clients a simple question: "On a scale of 0 to 10, how likely are you to recommend us to your friends and family?" Based on their answer, clients are divided into three categories: Promoters, Passives, and Detractors.

Promoters are clients who give a score of 9 or 10. Passives are those who give a score of 7 or 8. Detractors are those who give a score of 6 or lower.

Promoters should get monthly touches because they will actively refer you to new clients. Be sure to ask promoters for online reviews to spread the word and gain social proof of how great your team is.

Passive scores are opportunities to reach out and learn more about what could have made their experience better. What you learn will not only improve your company, it will also give the client a chance to give feedback. This lets them know that you care, which ultimately could be the deciding factor that may improve the score to a 9 or 10.

Detractors need to be approached immediately with an open and humble mindset. Do not avoid detractors because if they are left alone they will be a detriment to your goodwill and reputation in the community. You may not be able to win them over but, by showing them you care, you could move their score to passive. Because I haven't been afraid of detractors, even when I knew I was right and they were wrong, I still tried to mend the bridge to avoid downline consequences.

This score provides real-time insights into the experience of your clients and identifies areas that need improvement. By using NPS at critical points during the client's journey, teams can get an accurate picture of how their clients feel about the service they received, instead of relying on five-star reviews that may not accurately reflect their experience. By doing this, teams can identify any pain points that their clients may be experiencing and make changes to improve their overall experience.

Here are the most critical points to survey the client experience:

- **Initial Sales Conversation on a Recorded Line:** This is the first point of contact between your team and the potential client. It's important to survey their experience during this phase to understand how well your team is doing at making a positive first impression and to identify any areas for improvement. The survey is a simple check-in with the client from another person on the team. For example, our assistant may call the day after a listing appointment to see how the appointment went and if they have any questions. We may ask what was their key takeaway from the experience. Do they wish the agent would have done something differently? Do they believe the agent is the right person for the job?

- **Post-Appointment Review:** After an appointment with any team member, it's important to survey the client to understand what they thought of the appointment and to identify any areas that need improvement.

- **Post Review After Initial Showing:** After a buyer has seen a property for the first time, it's important to survey their experience to understand their thoughts on the property and to identify any areas for improvement in the showing process.

- **Post Review After Listing Appointment:** After a listing appointment, it's important to survey the client to understand what they thought of the appointment and to identify any areas for improvement in the listing process.

- **Post Under Contract:** After a contract has been signed, it's important to survey the client to understand how they feel about the contract process and to identify any areas for improvement.

- **Post Closing:** After the closing process is complete, it's important to survey the client experience to understand how they feel about the entire process and to identify any areas for improvement.

Another benefit of NPS is that it can be used to track the progress of your team over time. Teams can see if they are making improvements in the client experience and can measure the impact of any changes they have made.

By surveying the client and understanding their experience at these critical points, real estate teams can gain valuable insights into how their clients feel and make improvements to their overall experience. It's important to remember that the client's journey is ongoing and that teams should constantly be checking in on the client experience and making improvements.

So, as a real estate professional, it's time to start using NPS to understand the experience of your clients and to make improvements that will help you stand out from the competition.

DOMINATE SOCIAL PROOF

As humans, we have a tendency to look to others for guidance in our decision-making processes. This is what psychologist Robert Cialdini refers to as the principle of social proof in his book *Influence*. Social proof is a powerful tool in the world of real estate and understanding its importance can help your team take their customer experience to the next level.

Think about it. When you're considering purchasing a new product, you're more likely to do so if you see that others in your social circle have already made the same decision. The same can be said for the home-buying process. Prospective buyers are more likely to trust and feel confident in the services of a real estate team if they see that others they know have already had a positive experience with them.

Remember my very expensive sapphire? One person saying something meant very little. Two added credibility. Three pushed me over the edge. As humans, if we hear the same thing from at least three people, we are more likely to believe it.

This is why social proof is so important for real estate teams. By collecting and showcasing positive reviews and testimonials from previous clients, teams can demonstrate to potential clients that they have a proven track record of providing an exceptional experience.

Social proof can take many forms, from online reviews and testimonials to satisfied clients sharing their experience with their friends and family. By leveraging social proof, real estate teams can build trust and credibility with potential clients and increase their chances of closing the deal.

RUN REVIEW CONTESTS

One way we get reviews is by running a review contest. This is the contest we used to get 157 reviews in ten days. See the sample text below.

To: Real Estate Team
From: [Name of Sender]
Subject: Google Review Contest
Date: [Date of Memo]

Dear Team,

We are excited to announce that our Google Review Contest is back and it's better than ever. Our goal is to increase our online presence and improve our reputation by collecting as many positive reviews as possible on our Google page.

Contest Period: The contest will run from July 28th to August 6th, 2021.

Eligibility: All team members are eligible to participate in the contest.

Each team member can win the following prizes by collecting Google reviews:

- 1 Review - $5 Coffee Gift Card
- 5 Reviews - $150
- 10 Reviews - $250
- 20 Reviews - $500

In addition, if everyone on the team roster—including Kim, Kevin, Christina, etc.—gets at least one review, we will cater a very nice lunch the following week.

Contest Guidelines:

1. Participants are encouraged to reach out to friends, family, past clients, etc. to ask for a Google review.

2. The reviews don't have to be from first-hand experience, but 5-star reviews matter and should be accompanied by a written comment.
3. Participants should ask the reviewers to reference their name and the team in their review.
4. The link to our Google page can be found in the email below.

We are confident that this contest will be a great success and we appreciate your participation and contribution.

Please do not hesitate to reach out to [Name of Sender] if you have any questions.

Best regards,

[Name of Sender]

NEXT STEPS: HOW TO TURN LEADS INTO RAVING FANS

- The core concept of a raving fan is a client for life. When you change your mindset from a *one-time transaction* to *how do I protect and serve this person for life through real estate services*, it forces you to create long-term action processes.
- Take the time to build solid relationships with your clients and make them feel valued throughout the entire process.

You and your team need to get to know your clients on a personal level.

- The top reason people are dissatisfied with their agents is a lack of communication. When surveyed, buyers and sellers said they expected to hear from their agents daily. Keep your clients informed and updated at every stage of the buying or selling process. Use multiple communication channels, such as phone calls, emails, or texts, to ensure they are always in the loop and satisfied with the progress. The single most important action you can take to turn a client into a raving fan is to continue your communication and show you care after closing. Your competition will not and you will win.

- Develop training, so your team can be knowledgeable, empathetic, and proactive in addressing and resolving clients' concerns. A positive and supportive experience can turn leads into loyal fans. Everyone in the organization, including all the agents, should treat everyone's clients like their own. Have policies and standards in place on how your staff and agents should treat clients. You can control certain aspects of the client experience. For example, a staff member must greet everyone who walks into the office with a smile and say, "Hi, welcome to ABC Realty, how can I help you today?" Develop scripts for your staff on how to answer the phone, how to leave a voice message, and how to write an e-mail.

- Provide valuable educational content and resources for your clients, such as market reports, blog posts, or webinars, to help your clients make informed decisions. Have a weekly—or at a minimum, monthly—newsletter that is educational for all your past clients.

- Request feedback from your clients and use it to identify areas of improvement and opportunities for growth. This will show that you value their opinions and are committed to enhancing their experience. Clients become raving fans because they have a voice and you care about their opinions. When you get their opinions they become co-creators of your business and want to see you succeed.

- Organize events, workshops, or seminars for your clients to network. Create a VIP program where clients have access to professional services after closing, like a notary, moving truck, conference room, network of vendors, and contractor services.

- Create a referral program that rewards clients for recommending your team to others. This can help generate new leads and turn existing clients into raving fans. When you can serve a past client's friends and family at the highest level, that past client gets the validation from their friends and family for giving them a great reference. If you drop the ball on a referral, you can lose a client.

> **Framework:** Be sure to have a specific process for a client to refer someone else to your company. Build the process so the referral gets preferential treatment.

- Share client success stories—with permission!!!—on your website or social media channels. This can help build trust with potential clients and showcase your team's ability to deliver outstanding results.

- Maintain relationships with clients even after transactions are complete. Send periodic updates, congratulate them on anniversaries, or offer assistance with any future real estate needs. This will keep your team on their minds and encourage repeat business and referrals.

By focusing on the client experience and building a solid reputation, you will bring in more leads and close more business.

CHAPTER 17

BUILDING A DREAM TEAM

The art of recruiting top talent for your real estate business.

In this chapter, I will guide you through effective recruiting in the real estate world.

For years, I built my identity around being a hands-on leader. The image of me in the trenches, shoulder to shoulder with my team, was one I wore as a badge of honor. I was relentless, clocking in long hours and closing sales day after day. My performance was consistently at the top, so much so that I would remove my name from the leaderboard so that I didn't discourage my agents. I truly believed that leading by example was the way to inspire growth.

This approach took its toll. The pressure and stress of growing the business while also being an active salesperson demanded immense hours. I was always the first to arrive and the last to leave. I was determined to lead by example, but in reality, I had to work nonstop to keep things growing. This took a huge toll on my life.

It wasn't until I met Jon Cheplak that my perspective began to shift. He taught me that in order to elevate and step out of production, I needed to focus on growing the whole, trusting that the individual parts would follow suit. My previous approach was to concentrate on the growth of each person, assuming that if everyone improved, our sales would naturally grow. But Jon asked me a crucial question one day: "What do other agents outside your company say about your team?"

I paused, realizing that the answer was, "Probably nothing. We're a black box to them." And therein lay the problem. Nobody knew we were hiring, nobody knew we would hire them, and they certainly didn't know anything about our culture and what made us special. I had been so focused on working with my existing team members that I hadn't been letting the outside world see us.

That was the turning point for me. I decided to open the doors to our amazing culture and showcase the systems we had in place. Word began to spread and before I knew it our team tripled in size within the next 12 months. This new approach not only helped us attract top talent, but it also instilled a sense of pride and camaraderie among the team.

Now, I continue to lead by example, but in a different way. I dedicate myself to empowering and growing the entire team, rather than focusing solely on individual parts. Thanks to Jon Cheplak, I've come to understand the power of a united, motivated team, and the incredible impact that can have on the success of our business.

Looking back, I can't help but wonder how many opportunities I might have missed by keeping our company such a well-guarded secret. Opening up to the world has not only helped our team grow exponentially, but it has also allowed me to grow as a leader. I now know that by nurturing the whole, the parts will surely flourish, and together we will achieve greatness.

Recruiting, hiring, and attracting top talent is crucial to building a successful real estate team. As a leader, it's your responsibility to ensure that your team is composed of individuals who are not only skilled and knowledgeable but also passionate and motivated. To put it simply, look for people who have a strong appetite and aptitude for learning.

When building a real estate team, it's important to look beyond skills and experience. While those are important, they don't necessarily guarantee success. Instead, focus on finding individuals with a genuine passion for real estate, a strong work ethic, and a willingness to go the extra mile.

TOP TALENT

You know that having a top-notch sales team is key to success, but how do you find the right people to join your team? While traditional recruiting methods may work, there's a creative solution worth exploring, like in Chet Holmes' book *The Ultimate Sales Machine* you will find a Superstar's only ad.

Holmes' ad is designed to attract the best of the best salespeople, and it can be adapted for use in the real estate industry. By placing this ad, you'll attract only the most passionate, motivated, and driven individuals committed to excellence.

So what exactly does this ad say? In short, it calls for superstars, those who have a hunger for success and a drive to achieve their goals. It asks for individuals who are passionate about sales, who have a positive attitude, and who are willing to work hard to reach their goals. It also offers a glimpse into what makes your company unique and what sets it apart from the competition.

If you want superstar salespeople, your ad needs to target people who can make appointments from any starting position. You want to attract people who have what it takes to push through no matter what and can prove it.

During the interview, you must push your sales candidates to see if they can overcome rejection. During an interview, I might say something like "I'm not sure you have what it takes to..." I will then sit back and watch to see if they can overcome adversity. If they can't do this, they won't be able to overcome objections during the conversion or sales process.

THE COMPETITION

In the world of technology, giants like Google, Microsoft, and Facebook are always in a race to come up with the next big thing. While it might seem like they're in competition with each other, the truth is that they're all competing for the same thing: top talent. These tech giants know that the key to success lies in having the best and brightest minds working on their projects, and they're willing to do whatever it takes to attract and retain top talent.

Just as technology companies understand the importance of recruiting top talent, real estate teams must also realize the crucial role that recruiting and hiring plays in their success. After all, it's the agents on your team who are the face of your company, and they're the ones who are responsible for finding and closing deals.

To be successful, you need to have a strong team of agents who are motivated, knowledgeable, and skilled. And to attract and retain top talent, you must have a comprehensive recruiting and hiring program. This means spending time and resources on advertising and outreach efforts, as well as offering competitive compensation and benefits packages.

But it's not enough just to recruit top talent. Once you have them on your team, you need to support and develop them. This can include providing training and coaching opportunities, as well as creating a positive and supportive work environment. When your agents feel valued and supported, they're more likely to be motivated and engaged, which will translate into better results for your company.

If you want your real estate team to be successful, you need to prioritize recruiting and hiring. Spend time, money, and attention on finding the best and brightest agents, and provide them with the support and development opportunities they need to excel.

> **Framework:** Remember, top talent is the key to success, and investing in your team is an investment in your future.

SCHOLARSHIP PROGRAM

It's not always easy to attract top talent to the real estate industry. The perception of real estate as a high-risk low-reward career can be a major barrier for many people considering a career change. But what if there was a way to change that perception and open up the funnel for 10 times more applicants?

Enter the scholarship program. By offering to pay for online training, exam fee, and a spot on your team's onboarding and training program, you can attract high-level talent who might have otherwise overlooked the real estate industry.

Not only does this program make it easier for people to get started in the industry, but it also provides a supportive and structured path to success.

To start a scholarship program, you'll need to pre-interview potential scholarship recipients to make sure they have the skills and drive to succeed in real estate. Once you've identified the right candidates, you can offer them the scholarship and get started on your onboarding and training program. This can be done as a group with multiple scholarship recipients going through the program together. Not only does this provide a sense of community and support for the scholarship recipients, but it also makes the training process more efficient for your team.

> **Mastery:** One of the biggest benefits of offering a scholarship program is that it sets you apart from other real estate teams. By investing in your future agents, you're showing that you value their development and success. This not only sets the tone for a positive and supportive work environment, but it also helps to attract and retain top talent.

It's important to have a comprehensive onboarding and training program. This will help to ensure that the scholarship recipients have a strong foundation in the industry and are equipped with the skills they need to succeed. Additionally, providing ongoing coaching and support will help to keep them motivated and engaged, which will translate into better results for your team.

NEXT STEPS:
HOW TO BUILD YOUR DREAM TEAM

- Establish yourself as a thought leader in the local real estate industry by providing valuable and practical advice. This can be done through creating and sharing content on various platforms such as YouTube, social media, and email newsletters.

- Set up a rhythm by sharing real estate tips, tricks, and knowledge on a weekly basis. Consistency is the key to building credibility and maintaining an engaged audience. You need to be the most consistent leader in the industry. You have to be there when something goes wrong for other agents and they come to you for help and guidance.

- Communicate that your brokerage is hiring both new and experienced agents. This can be done through online advertisements and by ensuring that your website clearly states that you are recruiting. Everyone needs to know you are hiring at all times.

- Create a dedicated page or standalone website for potential agents to learn about your team, the benefits of joining, and fill out an application form. This will make the recruitment process more streamlined and efficient.

- Shoot video interviews with current team members to get their insights on what it's like to work with your brokerage. Share these testimonials on your website and social media platforms to give potential recruits an inside look at your team's culture.

- Organize and promote live events and training workshops for potential and licensed agents. Topics should be relevant and actionable, such as lead generation, negotiation, or other essential real estate skills. These events will showcase your brokerage's expertise and commitment to the growth of your agents.
- Invest in your team by holding social events and documenting these experiences through photos and videos. Sharing this content with your audience will give potential recruits a glimpse of your team's culture and camaraderie.
- Your recruiting budget should be equal to your new-listing-acquisition budget. This will demonstrate your commitment to growth and nurturing talent within your brokerage.
- Network with other industry professionals to identify potential recruits. Attend industry events and conferences to meet agents who may be considering changing their brokerage.
- Implement a referral program within your team. Encourage your existing agents to refer qualified candidates who may be interested in joining your brokerage. Offer incentives and rewards for successful referrals to motivate your team to actively participate in the recruitment process.

By following these actionable steps, you can effectively recruit both experienced agents and those who are considering obtaining their real estate license. Cultivating a strong, supportive, and skilled team will enable your brokerage to thrive and dominate the local market.

EXAMPLE OF SCHOLARSHIP ACCEPTANCE LETTER

Dear [Name],

We are thrilled to inform you that you have been accepted into our real estate scholarship program and onto our team here at the Nick McLean Real Estate Group. Your hard work and dedication to learning and growing in the industry have not gone unnoticed, and we believe that you have the potential to be a valuable addition to our team.

As a member of our team, you will have access to all of the resources and training opportunities that we have to offer, including reimbursement for your real estate course and one test attempt. We take our commitment to the overall quality and service of the industry very seriously, and we believe that our team members are the key to our success.

We have high expectations of all of our team members, and we believe that the program that you are entering will provide you with all of the skills, knowledge, and support that you need to be successful. The program includes required online licensing training, weekly progress reports, and a 6-week onboarding and productivity training. After the onboarding period, you will be expected to meet specific criteria, including prospecting and following up with a minimum of 25 contacts per week, role-playing with team members, providing leads for the listing department, maintaining a buyer inventory, and supporting our admin staff and listing department.

We are confident that with your dedication and hard work, you will thrive in this program and become a valuable team member. Please sign and date the agreement in the spaces provided and return it to us as soon as possible to acknowledge your acceptance of the terms of this scholarship agreement.

Sincerely,

Nick McLean
Chief Executive Officer
Nick McLean Real Estate Group

CHAPTER 18

THE FINANCIALS

A guide to understanding
and improving your
real estate business.

---

*In this chapter, we will discuss the importance
of monthly profit and loss statements,
gross revenues, break-even points, and more.*

As someone who was open to learning just about anything, I knew opening a real estate brokerage would be a challenge. But I never anticipated just how overwhelming it would be. I had to learn to navigate the various aspects of running a business, such as paying bills, collecting checks, leasing office space, creating marketing plans, and managing personnel.

I quickly realized that in order to hire agents and keep my business running smoothly, I needed to understand bookkeeping and accounting. My experience in college had taught me that accounting was an essential part of every business, but I had opted to pursue a career in flying rather than completing my accounting degree because when I visualized my life as an accountant it was not a life or career I was passionate about. I wanted adventure, risk, and rewards.

> **$1M:** It's true what they say: if you don't watch your money, someone else will.

Determined to master this aspect of the business, I purchased QuickBooks and set out to learn everything there was to know about it in a single weekend. After spending three hours absorbed in the software, I came to the stark realization that although I could learn the ins and outs of QuickBooks, I would be committing to doing this every weekend for the foreseeable future. That thought came with dread and regret, just like the time I imagined my life as an accountant.

That's when it hit me. There were people in the world who were born to do accounting, and they knew it much better than I ever could. As an entrepreneur, I needed to recognize when I was the weakest link and the bottleneck for growth in my business. Instead of stubbornly trying to learn something I would eventually dread, I decided to make a U-turn.

The following Monday, I called and interviewed three accounting firms, each offering bookkeeping, payroll, and accounting services. To my surprise, I found that I could outsource the work to a certified public accountant for less than what it would have cost me in time and energy—that doesn't even count the cost of mistakes I definitely would have made. I never looked back.

Since then, I've had a vendor partner handling my accounting needs, and each month, I review financials with what is essentially a CFO. My decision to outsource allowed me to focus on growing my real estate brokerage and eventually start five additional businesses. In each new venture, the first thing I do is meet with an accountant.

I've come a long way since 2012, and my willingness to learn has never waned, but the most important lesson I've taken away from my journey is that as an entrepreneur, it's crucial to recognize your own limitations and know when to delegate. In doing so, you give yourself the freedom to focus on what you're truly passionate about, and that's what ultimately leads to success.

You also need to embrace your monthly financials!

As a real estate agent, you're no stranger to hard work and hustle. But even the most driven people can find it challenging to stay on top of their finances. Between closing deals and growing your business, keeping track of the numbers can seem like a daunting task.

But the truth is, knowing your financials is important to the success of your business. It's the only way to ensure you're on the right track, making smart investments, and maximizing your profits.

The first step is to hire a bookkeeper and CPA firm to provide you with a monthly profit and loss statement. This statement will give you a snapshot of your financials for both the previous month and year-to-date, allowing you to see how you're doing and make any necessary adjustments.

But don't hide from the numbers! Embrace and analyze them. Use them to make informed decisions about your business. This is your opportunity to see where your money is going, what's working and what's not, and make changes that will help you reach your financial goals.

> **Mastery:** Until you reach over $5 million a year in revenue, it's best to outsource your bookkeeping, payroll, and financial reporting. Not only will this help to ensure that your financials are accurate and up-to-date, but it will also free up your time to focus on what you do

best-selling real estate. Once you reach over $5 million, you can consider hiring in-house accounting.

Don't let finances be a roadblock on your journey to success. Take control of your financials, and use the information you gather to grow your business and reach new heights. After all, a strong financial foundation is the key to a thriving real estate business.

So, go ahead, embrace your monthly financials and watch your business soar!

MAXIMIZING GROSS PROFIT

As a real estate team leader, you have a big responsibility on your shoulders. Not only do you have to manage your team, but you also have to ensure that your business is profitable. In order to do that, you have to know your numbers.

One of the most important numbers for a real estate business is the gross revenue produced by each team member. This number tells you how much revenue each member of your team is bringing in, and it's crucial to understanding the overall health of your business.

But gross revenue is only part of the equation. In order to truly understand your profits, you also need to know the cost of goods sold. This is the amount paid to each team member for each sale, and it's subtracted from your gross revenue to give you your gross profit—or the company retained dollars.

Your goal should always be to maximize your revenue-per-sale. The more revenue you bring in, the more money you have to cover your expenses and make a profit. And, as a wise businessman once said, there is no such thing as an unreasonable amount of profit. The goal of any business is to make a profit, and as a team leader, it's your responsibility to ensure that your business is profitable.

One way to maximize gross profit is to focus on your cost of goods sold. The cost of goods sold is most commonly the split the agent receives when they sell a home. Let's say your agent sells a home and receives 70% of the commission. The cost of goods sold is 70%. If you think about it another way, the company can never make more than 30% if all agents cost them 70% per sale. This is a common mistake I see when mentoring new teams. As a team leader, if you pay out too much per transaction (70%) and have to pay all the regular expenses and bills out of the remaining 30%, nothing is left to cover extra fees and bills—including your own salary — unless you personally stay in production. There are ways to increase your support and value to the agent where the cost of goods sold can go below 50%. Are there areas where you can cut costs and increase your profits? These are the questions you need to ask yourself in order to maximize your revenue per sale.

Another way to increase your gross profit is to focus on increasing your revenue. This can be done by closing more deals, selling more-expensive properties, or finding new ways to increase your sales.

As a real estate team leader, it's essential to understand your numbers. Knowing your gross revenue produced by each team member, as well as your cost of goods sold, is key to maximizing your gross profit and ensuring that your business is profitable.

THE BREAK-EVEN POINT

As a real estate team, it's essential to understand your finances, and one critical number to keep in mind is your break-even point. This is the number of sales you need to make in order to cover all of your expenses and not incur a loss.

To calculate your break-even point, you first need to determine your projected fixed expenses for the entire year. This includes expenses such as rent, labor, marketing, and other costs of running your business. Once you have that number, you need to calculate your gross profit per sale after you pay your agents.

Next, divide your fixed expenses by your gross profit per sale. The result is your break-even point; the exact number of sales you need to make to cover your expenses and not incur a loss. Let's take an average gross commission of $10,000. Your agent earns 50% or $5,000, resulting in a gross profit per sale of $5,000 to the company. When we look at our fixed expenses—labor, rent, marketing budget, etc.—we see $600,000 for the year. Taking our total fixed expenses and our gross profit per sale, we arrive at 120 sales to break even.

It's important to understand that you don't make a profit until you break even. This means that everything you do before that point is just covering your costs and keeping your business afloat.

You need to be strategic about your business decisions. You need to ensure that you're closing enough deals to reach your break-even point and make a profit. You also need to be mindful of your expenses and make sure that you're not overspending.

OFFSETTING EXPENSES

One way to stay on top of your finances is to offset your expenses with strategic marketing partners.

One example of a strategic marketing partner is a lender who can contribute directly to your advertising sources. This not only helps offset your expenses, but it also creates a strong partnership between your team and the lender.

> **$1M:** It's important to consult an attorney for legal compliance before entering into a marketing service agreement with any partner.

Another way to offset your expenses is by owning your own building and leasing space out to companies that want to be in close proximity to your team, such as lenders, title, escrow, inspectors, and insurers. If you don't own a building, you can still sublet space and use it for the same purpose.

It's important to always think critically about how you can get someone else to pay your expenses, especially promotions, events, and marketing. This is where the host-beneficiary strategy comes into play. By being a gracious host, you can offset all of your costs and maximize your marketing efforts.

Using this approach can be a game-changer for your business. It not only helps maximize your marketing efforts but also creates strong partnerships and provides opportunities for mutually beneficial relationships. So, be creative, think critically, and always look for ways to get others to contribute to your marketing efforts.

NEXT STEPS: HOW TO GET CONTROL OF THE FINANCIALS

- Hire a bookkeeper and CPA firm to provide you with a monthly profit and loss statement.
- Analyze your monthly financials and use them to make informed decisions about your business. This is your opportunity to see where your money is going, what's working, and what's not. Your CPA firm should provide these by email by the 10th of each month.
- Focus on maximizing gross profit by reducing the cost of goods sold and increasing your revenue.
- Calculate your break-even point. Share the results with your staff and team. That is your first goal and count down as you get closer and celebrate when you do.

- Offset expenses with strategic partners. You can do this by partnering with a lender who can contribute directly to your advertising sources or by subletting space to companies that want to be near your team. There are lenders who would love to pay 50% of your marketing costs.
- Use the host-beneficiary strategy: Always look for ways to get others to contribute to your marketing efforts. The host-beneficiary strategy involves being a gracious host and offsetting all of your costs to maximize your marketing efforts.

Don't let finances be a roadblock on your journey to success. Learn about the numbers, don't hide from them. Take control of your financials and use the information you gather to grow your business and reach new heights. After all, a strong financial foundation is key to a thriving real estate business.

CHAPTER 19

BUILDING A POWERFUL CULTURE

The key to unlocking your
team's potential.

---

*In this chapter, we will discuss how
you can create a positive work environment
through hiring acknowledgment,
community, and empowerment.*

In my first decade of running my real estate team, I attended countless conferences and exclusive masterminds where the most successful team leaders would reveal their closely-guarded secrets. Eager for growth and success, I paid to be in the right rooms with the right mastermind groups to learn from the wisdom that fueled these top teams. At times, I paid what would equate to a teacher's yearly salary to gain access to the right mentors and masterminds.

During these events, I noticed that there were two distinct types of advice. The first was about marketing: practical, results-driven strategies with clearly-connected dots. Implementing these strategies in our business made a tangible difference and helped us gain momentum.

But it was the second type of advice that proved to be the game-changer for my team: the discussions on culture. These conversations were different, more heartfelt, and introspective. The top teams would talk about emotions, feelings, and experiences within their organizations. The dots didn't seem to connect directly, but it was clear that the best teams had the best cultures.

These leaders raved about how their team members felt about the organization. They shared the pride they felt when their teams spoke highly of their experiences, never focusing on the number of homes sold but instead on the sense of belonging and fulfillment their team members experienced.

As I reflected on my own team's success, I realized that culture was the nucleus of our growth. It was this energy that attracted more agents and fueled more sales.

In our pursuit of success, I became convinced that everything is energy. It's either being depleted or enhanced, and our team's culture was an energy that enhanced the group.

Over the years, I poured my heart into creating a stronger culture for our team, a place where people felt connected, inspired, and motivated. And as our culture grew, so did our success. The lessons I learned from those top team leaders forever shaped the way I approached my business, with culture at the center of it all.

As Daniel Coyle says in his book *The Culture Code*, "Culture is not the buttress of a structure; it is the structure itself." Your team's culture is the foundation upon which everything else is built, and it is up to you to create and maintain a positive and thriving environment.

Hiring and firing to the culture is essential. When you bring new team members on board, make sure they fit with your team's values and beliefs. And when someone no longer aligns with your team's culture, it's time to let them go. It may be tough, but it is crucial to preserving the integrity of your team's culture.

People crave meaningful work. It's what makes them feel fulfilled and satisfied with their jobs. This is why it's so important to ensure that your team is working toward a common goal, a shared mission that everyone can be proud of. People want to contribute, to make a difference, and to be a part of something bigger than themselves. And they want to be part of a community, a group of people who share their values and beliefs. This is why it's so important to create opportunities for your team to bond, both online and offline.

Finally, give your team control of their own time. People want to feel empowered, and they want to know that they have the freedom to make decisions that affect their work and their lives. This is why it's so important to provide them with the tools and resources they need to communicate, bond, and grow together and then let them do it.

NEXT STEPS:
HOW TO CREATE A POWERFUL CULTURE

- As the leader, your team needs to know what you expect from them and how you will acknowledge them for doing a good job. To do this, set clear expectations. Each team member must understand their role and responsibilities and why they matter within the collective.

- Foster an environment where team members feel comfortable sharing their ideas, concerns, and challenges without fear of judgment or criticism. Regularly scheduled team meetings, one-on-one check-ins, and opportunities for feedback. Always think of ways to get the group to say what they need. Develop leaders within your team who can run a meeting or training. Find people doing the right things, bring them to the front, and have them share what works for them.

- Trust is the foundation of any strong team bond. Encourage honesty, transparency, and accountability among team members. Address any issues openly and promptly to maintain trust. Send out a quarterly team survey asking for feedback on how the team can improve. Share the results with the team and let them know why you are or are not going to make a change based on their feedback. They need to know they have a voice and are co-creators in the business. If they feel they have an impact on the direction of the team, they will be more satisfied in their jobs and work harder for the overall success.

- Organize regular team-building activities, such as workshops, games, or offsite retreats, to foster connections and relationships. Once a month—or quarterly at a minimum—have a team activity outside of the office that has nothing to do with real estate. This could be a BBQ at the park, Top Golf, bowling, painting, hiking, etc. Your team will forge bonds outside of work that will create better inclusivity and trust.

- Regularly acknowledge and celebrate individual and team successes. Your team eagerly wants to know they are doing a good job and, as a leader, you need to continually look for people doing the right things. Nobody is inspired by a leader who carries around a to-do list and is constantly pointing out errors. Celebrate your team members privately and publicly.

- Encourage team members to develop new skills and take on new challenges. Provide resources, training, and support to help them grow professionally and personally. Don't discourage agents and team members from exploring new licenses and designations.

> **$1M:** There is no training or certification I won't pay for my team to get, and I often reward them by investing in their most valuable asset, their brain.

- Promote a healthy personal life by setting reasonable expectations, offering flexible work arrangements, and encouraging team members to take breaks and time off when needed. How can you elevate the stress, anxiety, and fear they may experience at home? Have a fund that can go to team members in need. We all fall on hard times and sometimes they pile up. There will be times when you can help someone in need.

- As a leader, demonstrate the values and behaviors you want to see in your team. Be transparent, approachable, and empathetic, and always strive for continuous improvement. Be vulnerable as a leader and share your own stories of making mistakes, experiencing fear, or feeling anxiety. It is much harder, and unsustainable, to pretend to be perfect in front of your team. You are human and they will connect with you more if you share who you truly are.

Building a powerful culture is the key to unlocking your team's potential and achieving long-term success. By creating an environment where agents can choose to be productive and contribute to the greater whole and the communities they serve, you will build life value into your team's employment. Implement the strategies in this chapter to set clear expectations, encourage open communication, develop trust, organize team-building activities, recognize achievements, and provide growth opportunities.

CONCLUSION

THE WRAP-UP

It's time to start building your million-dollar business.

Congratulations on making it through *Million Dollar Agent.* I hope you have gained insights and ideas that will help you transform your real estate business.

The concepts presented in this book are not just a theory; they are real-world, in-the-trenches, proven steps that have been tested and refined over time. Whether you're a solo agent or team leader, this book has provided you with the fundamental principles to build a successful and profitable real estate team.

But knowledge alone is not enough. You must choose to take action and implement these strategies in your business. You must be willing to put in the hard work and dedication necessary to create the most profitable real estate team in your marketplace.

Know that in business, even with a playbook, it is a process and there will always be a learning curve. Things take longer than expected and require more effort than you anticipate. The road to success is not easy, but it is achievable. It requires discipline, focus, and commitment to follow the steps laid out in this book. It may not happen overnight, but if you stay the course, you will see the results you desire.

It's easy to feel great at the end of a conference or class. You go back to your office on fire and ready to implement everything! But within a week, everything is back to the standard day-in-day-out. Decide now, what are you going to do to not fall back into your comfortable routine. What will you do next Monday? Next month? Make that plan now so you can keep the fire and not forget all those aha moments. Use the tools, strategies, and frameworks you've learned in this book and implement them. Don't let fear or doubt hold you back. Take the first step today and begin your journey to success.

I believe in you and wish you all the best on your journey to building a successful and profitable real estate team.

Thank you for reading this book. If you enjoyed it, share it with a friend. You can also connect with me on social media and my website.

REFERENCES

Cialdini, R., (1984). *Influence: How and Why People Agree to Things*. William Morrow & Co.

Collins, J., (2011). *Good to Great: Why Some Companies Make the Leap...And Others Don't*. Harper Business.

Collins, J., & Lazier, W., (2020). *BE 2.0: Turning Your Business into an Enduring Great Company*. Random House Business.

Collins, J., Porras, J., (2004). *Built to Last: Successful Habits of Visionary Companies*. Harper Business.

Coyle, D., (2018). *The Culture Code: The Secrets of Highly Successful Groups*. Bantam.

Coyle, D., (2009). *The Talent Code: Greatness Isn't Born. It's Grown. Here's How*. Bantam.

Godin, S., (2003). *Purple Cow: Transform Your Business by Being Remarkable*. Portfolio.

Godin, S., (2007). *The Dip: A Little Book That Teaches You When to Quit (and When to Stick)*. Portfolio.

Godin, S., (2018). *This Is Marketing: You Can't Be Seen Until You Learn to See*. Portfolio.

Holmes, C., (2007). *The Ultimate Sales Machine: Turbocharge Your Business with Relentless Focus on 12 Key Strategies.* Portfolio.

Jantsch, J., (2007). *Duct Tape Marketing: The World's Most Practical Small Business Marketing Guide.* Nelson Business.

Maddox, J., & West, B., (2019). *Call Sign Chaos: Learning to Lead.* Random House.

Manning, H., Bodine, K., & Bernoff, J., (2012). *Outside In: The Power of Putting Customers at the Center of Your Business.* Houghton Mifflin Harcourt.

Maxwell, J., (2011). *The 5 Levels of Leadership: Proven Steps to Maximize Your Potential.* Evonature.

Miller, D., (2017). *Building a StoryBrand: Clarify Your Message So Customers Will Listen.* HarperCollins Leadership.

Pink, D., (2009). *Drive: The Surprising Truth About What Motivates Us.* Riverhead Books.

ABOUT THE AUTHOR

Nick McLean is an executive-level real estate broker. His team sells more than 500 homes and produces over $250,000,000 in sales volume annually. Through his years of trial and error and high-value education, he has discovered what it takes to build and maintain his position as an industry leader. He not only passes on his knowledge as an elite real estate coach with Jon Cheplak's Select Coaching, but he also provides his own team with training sessions each morning and numerous opportunities to expand their credentials and professional development.

Nick McLean is also a former wildland firefighter and trained Boeing 747 pilot. He prides himself on clocking out at 11 a.m. so he can be a devoted father, husband, and Competitive XC Mountain Bike Racer.

Nick wrote *Million Dollar Agent* to share his business acumen with everyone.

Friend Nick on **Facebook** at
www.facebook.com/nickmcleanrealestate

Check Nick's **tutorials** at
www.youtube.com/@nickmcleanreal

Contact Nick for **coaching** at
www.mcleancoaching.com

Catch up with Nick on **Instagram** at
www.instagram.com/nickmcleanre

Follow Nick on **Twitter**
@nickmcleanre

Made in the USA
Middletown, DE
15 August 2024

59174900R00135

Sex Tips

From Women who Ride the Sexual Frontier

Jo-Anne Baker

First published in Great Britain by Fusion Press,
a division of Satin Publications Ltd., London

This book is copyright under the Berne Convention.
All rights reserved. No part of this publication may be reproduced,
stored in a retrieval system, or transmitted in any form or by any
means, electronic, mechanical, photocopying, recording or
otherwise, without prior written permission of the publisher.

Fusion Press
20 Queen Anne Street
London W1M 0AY
E-mail: sheenadewan@compuserve.com
website: http://www.visionpaperbacks.demon.co.uk

Cover Image: ©2000 Nickolai Globe
Layout: Justine Hounam
Printed and bound in Great Britain by Biddles Ltd.

© Jo-Anne Baker
ISBN: 1-901250-73-3